BEGINNING SWIFT™ PROGRA

MW01154966

BEGINNING

Swift™ Programming

BEGINNING

Swift™ Programming

Wei-Meng Lee

Beginning Swift™ Programming

Published by
John Wiley & Sons, Inc.
10475 Crosspoint Boulevard
Indianapolis, IN 46256
www.wiley.com

Copyright © 2015 by John Wiley & Sons, Inc., Indianapolis, Indiana

Published simultaneously in Canada

ISBN: 978-1-119-00931-3
ISBN: 978-1-119-04288-4 (ebk)
ISBN: 978-1-119-00932-0 (ebk)

Manufactured in the United States of America

10 9 8 7 6 5 4 3 2 1

Limit of Liability/Disclaimer of Warranty: The publisher and the author make no representations or warranties with respect to the accuracy or completeness of the contents of this work and specifically disclaim all warranties, including without limitation warranties of fitness for a particular purpose. No warranty may be created or extended by sales or promotional materials. The advice and strategies contained herein may not be suitable for every situation. This work is sold with the understanding that the publisher is not engaged in rendering legal, accounting, or other professional services. If professional assistance is required, the services of a competent professional person should be sought. Neither the publisher nor the author shall be liable for damages arising herefrom. The fact that an organization or Web site is referred to in this work as a citation and/or a potential source of further information does not mean that the author or the publisher endorses the information the organization or Web site may provide or recommendations it may make. Further, readers should be aware that Internet Web sites listed in this work may have changed or disappeared between when this work was written and when it is read.

For general information on our other products and services please contact our Customer Care Department within the United States at (877) 762-2974, outside the United States at (317) 572-3993 or fax (317) 572-4002.

Wiley publishes in a variety of print and electronic formats and by print-on-demand. Some material included with standard print versions of this book may not be included in e-books or in print-on-demand. If this book refers to media such as a CD or DVD that is not included in the version you purchased, you may download this material at http://booksupport.wiley.com. For more information about Wiley products, visit www.wiley.com.

Library of Congress Control Number: 2014951015

Trademarks: Wiley, the Wiley logo, Wrox, the Wrox logo, Programmer to Programmer, and related trade dress are trademarks or registered trademarks of John Wiley & Sons, Inc. and/or its affiliates, in the United States and other countries, and may not be used without written permission. Swift is a trademark of Apple, Inc. All other trademarks are the property of their respective owners. John Wiley & Sons, Inc., is not associated with any product or vendor mentioned in this book. *Beginning Swift Programming* is an independent publication has not been authorized, sponsored, or otherwise approved by Apple, Inc.

To my family:

Thanks for your understanding and support while I worked on getting this book ready. I could not have done this without your help!

I love you all!

ABOUT THE AUTHOR

WEI-MENG LEE is a technologist and founder of Developer Learning Solutions (`www.learn2develop.net`), a technology company specializing in hands-on training on the latest mobile technologies. Wei-Meng has many years of training experience, and his training courses place special emphasis on the learning-by-doing approach. This hands-on approach to learning programming makes understanding the subject much easier than reading books, tutorials, and other documentation.

Wei-Meng is also the author of *Beginning iOS 5 Application Development* (Wrox, 2010) and *Beginning Android 4 Application Development* (Wrox, 2011). Contact Wei-Meng at `weimenglee@learn2develop.net`.

ABOUT THE TECHNICAL EDITOR

CHAIM KRAUSE is a Simulation Specialist at the US Army's Command and General Staff College, where he develops various software products on a multitude of platforms, from iOS and Android devices to Windows desktops and Linux servers, among other duties. Python is his preferred language, but he is multilingual and also codes in Java and JavaScript/HTML5/CSS, and others. He was fortunate to begin his professional career in the software field at Borland, where he was a Senior Developer Support Engineer for Delphi. Outside of computer geek stuff, Chaim enjoys techno and dubstep music and scootering with his two sled dogs, Dasher and Minnie.

CREDITS

Executive Editor
Robert Elliott

Project Editor
John Sleeva

Technical Editor
Chaim Krause

Production Editor
Christine Mugnolo

Copy Editor
Luann Rouff

Production Manager
Kathleen Wisor

**Manager of Content Development
and Assembly**
Mary Beth Wakefield

Marketing Director
David Mayhew

Marketing Manager
Carrie Sherrill

**Professional Technology &
Strategy Director**
Barry Pruett

Business Manager
Amy Knies

Associate Publisher
Jim Minatel

Project Coordinator, Cover
Patrick Redmond

Proofreader
Nancy Carrasco

Technical Proofreader
Matthew Eccles

Indexer
Robert Swanson

Cover Designer
Wiley

Cover Image
© iStock.com/Gorfer

ACKNOWLEDGMENTS

I WANT TO TAKE this chance to thank some key people who worked very hard behind the scenes to make this book a reality.

First, a big "thank you" to Bob Elliott, executive editor at Wrox. When I proposed this book to Bob, his first question was, how fast can you do it? And the rest, as they say, is history. Thank you, Bob, for the confidence you had in me to deliver this book on time!

Of course, I cannot forget John Sleeva, my editor (and a new friend!), who is always a pleasure to work with. Thank you, John, for the guidance and encouragement to keep the project going!

I am also grateful to my technical editors, Chaim Krause and Matthew Eccles. Chaim has never failed to spot my mistakes in the manuscript, and I can always count on him to give suggestions on how to improve the code. Thanks, Chaim! Matthew has also been eagle-eye testing my code samples to ensure that they work with the latest release of Xcode. Thanks, Matthew!

Last but not least, I want to take this chance to thank my family. The fact that you are holding this book in your hand is the result of the help I received while working on this book. I want to thank my wife, Sze Wa, for taking care of Chloe, our new baby, while I was rushing to meet the deadlines. She has been selflessly taking care of Chloe after her delivery, and I know it is physically and psychologically draining for her. Thank you, dear!

Our parents have also been extremely helpful in taking turns to help take care of our baby during the periods where I have to juggle between work, travelling, and writing. They have done so without any complaints, and for this I am deeply grateful. I would like to say to our parents and family: I love you all! Finally, to our lovely dog, Ookii, thanks for faithfully staying by our side.

CONTENTS

INTRODUCTION

THE IT WORLD IS an extremely fast-changing one. Small changes occur nearly daily, and every now and then something big happens that changes the entire industry, if not the world. For example, the iPhone, introduced in 2007, transformed the mobile industry overnight, spearheading the new era of the smartphones. The launch of the iPad three years later (2010) changed the way we use our computers, causing many to predict that we are all entering the end of the PC era.

For a long time after its inception in the 1980s, Objective-C was used by NeXT for its NeXTStEP operating system. Mac OS X and iOS both derived from NeXTSTEP, and Objective-C was thus the natural choice of language to use for Mac OS and iOS development. Developers starting on iOS development often complain that Objective-C does not look like a modern programming language (such as Java or C#), and that it is difficult to write and requires spending significant amounts of time trying to learn. For seven years, Apple has improved on the language and the iOS framework, making life easier for developers by introducing helpful features, such as Automatic Reference Counting (ARC), which takes the drudgery out of memory management, and Storyboard, which simplifies the flow of your application user interface. However, this did not stop all the complaints. Furthermore, Apple needed a new language that could take iOS and Mac OS development to the next level.

In 2014, at the Apple World Wide Developers Conference (WWDC), Apple took many developers by surprise by introducing a new programming language: Swift. After seven years, Apple finally released a new language that can replace Objective-C! As you will see throughout this book, Swift is a modern programming language with an easy-to-read syntax, and strict enforcement of type safety.

This book was written with busy developers in mind. It aims to cut through all the technical jargon and dive straight into the language. Of course, the best way to learn any new language is to see code examples, and this book is loaded with them. To get the most from the material, therefore, I strongly recommend that you work through the examples in each chapter as you read them.

WHO THIS BOOK IS FOR

This book is targeted at both beginning iOS developers and experienced Objective-C developers. It assumes a foundation in programming, and an understanding of object-oriented programming (OOP) concepts is required to get the most out of this book.

All the code samples in the chapters were written and tested using the final version of Xcode 6. Because the Swift language is still evolving, expect to see minor tweaks by the time this book is on the market.

HOW THIS BOOK IS STRUCTURED

This book covers the key topics of Swift programming using Xcode 6. It is divided into the following 12 chapters:

Chapter 1, "Introduction to Swift," covers the basic syntax of Swift and how to set up the development environment so that you can test your Swift code.

Chapter 2, "Data Types," covers the basic data types supported in Swift and how to perform the common operations involving them. It also covers the new tuple and optional data types introduced in Swift.

Chapter 3, "Strings and Characters," discusses how strings and characters are managed in Swift. In particular, special emphasis is placed on how the string type in Swift is backwardly compatible with the NSString in Objective-C. Also covered are things you need to be aware of when dealing with Unicode characters.

Chapter 4, "Basic Operators," covers all the commonly used operators supported by Swift. In addition, it discusses the new range operators introduced in Swift.

Chapter 5, "Functions," explains how functions are defined in Swift and the use of internal and external parameter names when calling them.

Chapter 6, "Collections," covers the collection types supported in Swift—arrays and dictionaries.

Chapter 7, "Control Flow and Looping," covers how to make decisions in Swift and how to use the looping statements to execute your Swift code repetitively.

Chapter 8, "Structures and Classes," covers the basics of these programming constructs. It also demonstrates how to define properties and methods in your classes and structures.

Chapter 9, "Inheritance," covers how to create subclasses in Swift and how access control rules affect the accessibility of a member. It also explains how to extend a class using the extension feature.

Chapter 10, "Closures," covers everything you need to know about these blocks of functionality and demonstrates how they enable you to write versatile code in Swift.

Chapter 11, "Protocols and Delegates," discusses a very important part of Swift's design pattern. The protocol and delegate model is the basis on which most of the APIs in iOS and Mac OS programming are based.

Chapter 12, "Generics," covers how Swift embraces this familiar programming concept, which enables the developer to write highly adaptable code that promotes sharing and reusing.

The appendix offers the answers to the exercises found at the end of each chapter.

WHAT YOU NEED TO USE THIS BOOK

In order to follow the examples provided in this book, you need a Mac to install Xcode 6. Xcode 6 is available for download, free, from the Mac App Store. No iOS device is needed to test the code in this book. For testing, you can create either a Playground project or an iOS project, which you can then test on the included iPhone Simulator.

CONVENTIONS

To help you get the most from the text and keep track of what's happening, we've used a number of conventions throughout the book.

> **NOTE** Notes indicates notes, tips, hints, tricks, and asides to the current discussion.

> **WARNING** Warnings hold important, not-to-be-forgotten information that is directly relevant to the surrounding text.

As for styles in the text:

➤ We *highlight* new terms and important words when we introduce them.

➤ We show keyboard strokes like this: Command+A.

➤ We show file names, URLs, and code within the text like so: `persistence.properties`.

We present code in two different ways:

```
We use a monofont type with no highlighting for most code examples.
We use bold to emphasize code that is particularly important in the present context
or to show changes from a previous code snippet.
```

SOURCE CODE

As you work through the examples in this book, you should type all the code into Xcode and observe the results. Remember, the best way to learn a language is to experience it yourself and make mistakes. For Chapter 11, you can find the source code for the LBS project at www.wrox/com/go/beginningswift. When at the site, simply locate the book's title (use the Search box or one of the title lists) and click the Download Code link on the book's detail page to obtain all the source code for the book.

After you download the code, just decompress it with your favorite compression tool. Alternatively, go to the main Wrox code download page at www.wrox.com/dynamic/books/download.aspx to see the code available for this book and all other Wrox books.

> **NOTE** *Because many books have similar titles, you may find it easiest to search by ISBN; this book's ISBN is 978-1-119-00931-3.*

ERRATA

We make every effort to ensure that there are no errors in the text or in the code. However, no one is perfect, and mistakes do occur. If you find an error in one of our books, such as a spelling mistake or a faulty piece of code, we would be very grateful for your feedback. By sending in errata, you may save another reader hours of frustration and at the same time help us provide even higher-quality information.

To find the errata page for this book, go to www.wrox.com and locate the title using the Search box or one of the title lists. Then, on the book details page, click the Book Errata link. On this page, you can view all errata that has been submitted for this book and posted by Wrox editors. A complete book list, including links to each book's errata, is also available at www.wrox.com/misc-pages/booklist.shtml.

If you don't spot "your" error on the Book Errata page, go to www.wrox.com/contact/techsupport.shtml and complete the form there to send us the error you have found. We'll check the information and, if appropriate, post a message to the book's errata page and fix the problem in subsequent editions of the book.

P2P.WROX.COM

For author and peer discussion, join the P2P forums at p2p.wrox.com. The forums are a web-based system for you to post messages relating to Wrox books and related technologies and to interact with other readers and technology users. The forums offer a subscription feature to e-mail you topics of interest of your choosing when new posts are made to the forums. Wrox authors, editors, other industry experts, and your fellow readers are present on these forums.

At p2p.wrox.com, you will find a number of different forums that will help you not only as you read this book but also as you develop your own applications. To join the forums, just follow these steps:

1. Go to p2p.wrox.com and click the Register link.

2. Read the terms of use and click Agree.

3. Complete the required information to join as well as any optional information you want to provide and click Submit.

4. You will receive an e-mail with information describing how to verify your account and complete the joining process.

> **NOTE** You can read messages in the forums without joining P2P, but in order to post your own messages, you must join.

After you join, you can post new messages and respond to messages that other users post. You can read messages at any time on the web. If you want to have new messages from a particular forum e-mailed to you, click the Subscribe to This Forum icon by the forum name in the forum listing.

For more information about how to use the Wrox P2P, be sure to read the P2P FAQs for answers to questions about how the forum software works, as well as for many common questions specific to P2P and Wrox books. To read the FAQs, click the FAQ link on any P2P page.

1

Introduction to Swift

WHAT YOU WILL LEARN IN THIS CHAPTER:

➤ What Swift is

➤ Why Swift is important

➤ Setting up the development environment to learn Swift

➤ How to create a Playground project

➤ How to create an iOS project

➤ The syntax of Swift

➤ How to declare constants

➤ How to declare variables

➤ Using string interpolation to include variable values in strings

➤ Swift statements

➤ How to print the values of variables for debugging

➤ How to insert comments in your Swift code

Apple surprised the Mac and iOS developer world at the Apple World Wide Developers Conference (WWDC) 2014 with the announcement of a new programming language: Swift. The aim of Swift is to replace Objective-C with a much more modern language syntax without worrying too much about the constraints of C compatibility. Apple itself touted Swift as Objective-C without the C.

For developers already deeply entrenched in Objective-C, it is foreseeable that Objective-C will still be the supported language for iOS and Mac OS X development in the near and immediate future. However, signs are all pointing to Apple's intention to make Swift the future language of choice for iOS and Mac development.

In this chapter, you will learn about the basics of Swift and how you can set up the development environment to learn it.

WHAT IS SWIFT?

Swift is a new programming language designed by Apple for Cocoa (Mac OS X) and Cocoa Touch (iOS) programming. The syntax of Swift is similar to modern languages such as Java and C#, while at the same time retaining some of the core features of Objective-C, such as named parameters, protocols, and delegates. The language's clear syntax makes your code simpler to read and maintain.

As an example, consider the following method in Objective-C:

```
-(int) addOneNumber:(int) num1 withAnotherNum:(int) num2
{
    return num1 + num2;
}
```

The preceding method adds two numbers and returns their sum. To use the method, you can pass a message to it:

```
int sum = [self addOneNumber:2 withAnotherNum:7];
```

Note the verbosity of Objective-C and the use of named parameters in the method name. The following example shows the same method in Swift:

```
func addTwoNumbers(num1:Int, num2:Int) -> Int {
    return num1 + num2
}
```

The preceding statements define a function called `addTwoNumbers`, accept two arguments, and return an integer value. You can call the method like this:

```
var sum = addTwoNumbers(2,5)
```

As you can see, Swift's syntax is simpler and easier to read.

In keeping with Objective-C's named parameters tradition, you can also use named parameters in methods:

```
func addTwoNumbers(num1:Int, secondNumber num2:Int) -> Int {
    return num1 + num2
}
```

You can now call the method using named parameters:

```
var sum = addTwoNumbers(2, secondNumber:5)
```

> **NOTE** *Chapter 5 discusses functions and named parameters in more detail.*

Swift is also designed to be a type-safe language. Variables must be initialized before use. In most cases, you have to perform explicit type conversions when assigning values from one type to another. Also, variables that are not assigned a value cannot be used in a statement and will be flagged as errors.

In Swift, for safety reasons there is no implicit type conversion—you must explicitly convert an Int to a Float (or Double). For example, you cannot implicitly assign an Int variable to a Float variable:

```
var f:Float
var i:Int = 5
f = i  //---error---
```

Rather, you need to explicitly convert the value into a Float value:

```
f = Float(i)
```

> **NOTE** *Chapter 2 discusses data types in more detail.*

WHY SWIFT IS IMPORTANT

Make no mistake; Apple did not create Swift for the sake of creating a new programming language. With the platform wars heating up, Apple desperately needs a language that will enable it to secure its long-term lead in the mobile platform market. Swift is strategic to Apple in a number of ways:

➤ It fixes many of the issues developers had with Objective-C—particularly, that Objective-C is hard to learn—replacing it with a language that is both fast to learn and easy to maintain.

➤ It delivers this easy-to-learn language while retaining the spirit of Objective-C but without its verbose syntax.

➤ It is a much safer language than Objective-C, which contributes to a much more robust app platform.

➤ It is able to coexist with Objective-C, which gives developers ample time to port their code to Swift over time.

SETTING UP THE ENVIRONMENT

To test all the Swift examples in this book, you need a Swift compiler. The easiest way to obtain the Swift compiler is to download the Xcode 6 from the Mac App Store (see Figure 1-1).

Once Xcode 6 is downloaded and installed on your Mac, launch it (see Figure 1-2).

There are two ways to test the code in this book:

➤ **Create a Playground project**—Playground is a new feature in Xcode 6 that makes learning Swift easy and fun. As you enter each line of code, Playground will evaluate the line and display the results. You can also use it to watch the values of variables as you step through the code. Playground is very useful for examining variable types when you are assigning values to them.

➤ **Create an iOS project**—You can create an iOS project and test your application using the iPhone Simulator included in the Xcode 6. While the focus of this book is on the Swift programming language and not iOS development, testing your code in an iOS project enables you to test your code in its entirety.

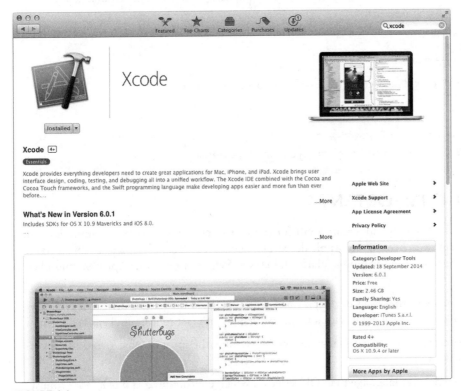

FIGURE 1-1

Creating a Playground Project

To create a Playground project, launch Xcode 6 and select File ➪ New ➪ Playground.... Name the Playground project and select the platform you want to test it on (see Figure 1-3).

Once the Playground project is created, you will see the editor shown in Figure 1-4. You can start writing your Swift code in this editor. I will show you some of Playground's neat features as we discuss the various Swift topics covered in this chapter.

For example, consider the following code snippet:

```
var sum = 0
for index in 1...5 {
    sum += index
}
```

The preceding code snippet sums all the numbers from 1 to 5. If you type this code snippet into Playground, you will see that the right side of the Playground window displays a circle (see Figure 1-5).

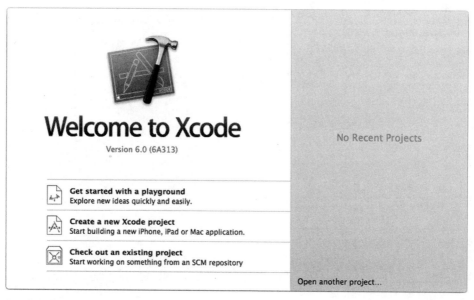

FIGURE 1-2

FIGURE 1-3

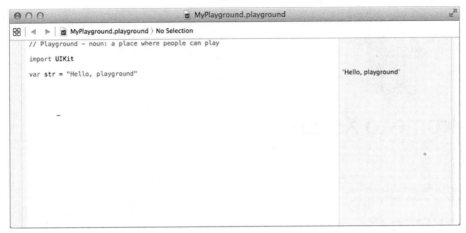

FIGURE 1-4

```
var sum = 0                        0
for index in 1...5 {
    sum += index                   (5 times)
}
```

FIGURE 1-5

Clicking on the circle will reveal the Timeline, where you can examine the values for sum for each iteration of the For loop (see Figure 1-6).

This feature makes it very easy for you to trace through your code, and it is especially useful when you are analyzing your new algorithm.

> **NOTE** *The For loop is discussed in more detail in Chapter 7.*

Creating an iOS Project

An alternative to creating a Playground project is to create an iOS project. In Xcode 6, select File ➪ New ➪ Project… and you will see the dialog shown in Figure 1-7.

Select Application under the iOS category (on the left) and then select the Single View Application template. Click Next.

> **NOTE** *The Single View Application template creates an iPhone project with a single View window. This is the best template to use for learning Swift without getting bogged down with how an iOS application works.*

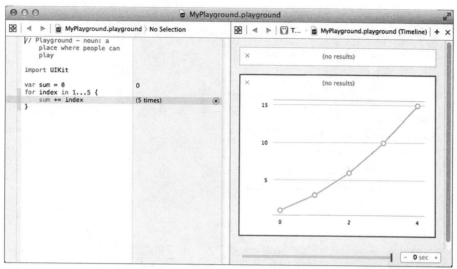

FIGURE 1-6

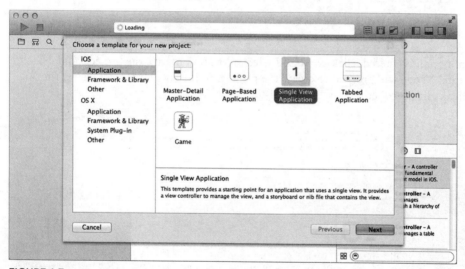

FIGURE 1-7

In the next dialog, enter the information as follows (see Figure 1-8):

➤ **Product Name**—The name of the project.

➤ **Organization Name**—This can either be your name or your organization's name.

➤ **Organization Identifier**—Commonly the reverse domain name of your company. If your organization's domain name were example.com, then you would enter com.example. The Organization Identifier and the Product Name are concatenated to form a unique string called the Bundle Identifier. Every application listed on the App Store must have a unique Bundle Identifier. For testing purposes, this is not important.

➤ **Language**—Select Swift.

➤ **Devices**—Select iPhone.

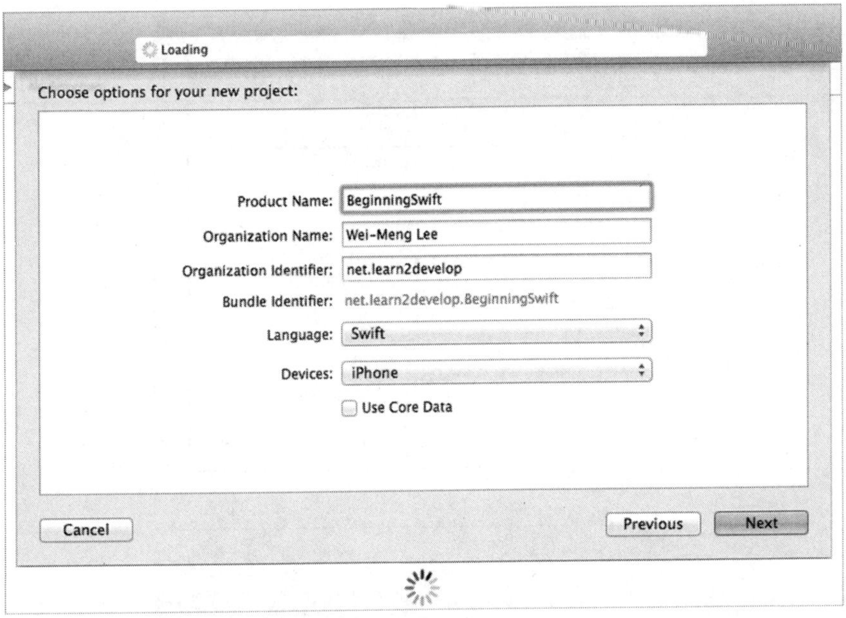

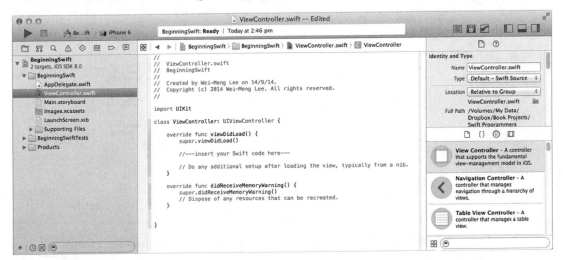

FIGURE 1-8

Once the information is entered, click Next and select a location to save the project, and then click Create. Xcode will proceed to create the project. In the created project, select the ViewController.swift file for editing (see Figure 1-9).

FIGURE 1-9

To test your Swift code, you can insert it in the position indicated in bold in the following example:

```
import UIKit

class ViewController: UIViewController {

    override func viewDidLoad() {
```

```
        super.viewDidLoad()

        //---insert your Swift code here---
        println("Hello, Swift!")

        // Do any additional setup after loading the view, typically from a
        // nib.
    }

    override func didReceiveMemoryWarning() {
        super.didReceiveMemoryWarning()
        // Dispose of any resources that can be recreated.
    }
}
```

To run the application, select the iPhone 6 Simulator and click the Build and Run button (see Figure 1-10). Alternatively, you can also use the Command+R keyboard shortcut.

FIGURE 1-10

You should now see the iPhone Simulator appear (see Figure 1-11).

FIGURE 1-11

As our focus in this book is not on iOS programming, you would be primarily interested in the output generated by your Swift code. Back in Xcode 6, press Command+Shift+C to reveal the Output window. Figure 1-12 shows our single Swift code printing out a line in the Output window.

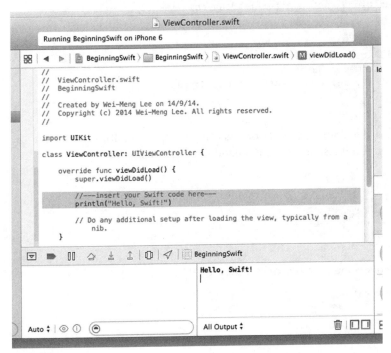

FIGURE 1-12

SWIFT SYNTAX

Now that you know how to set up the development environment for learning Swift and have looked at the various types of projects you can create to experiment with it, this section introduces the various syntaxes of Swift, beginning with how to create constants and variables.

Constants

In Swift, you create a constant using the `let` keyword:

```
let radius = 3.45
let numOfColumns = 5
let myName = "Wei-Meng Lee"
```

Notice that there is no need to specify the data type—they are inferred automatically. In the preceding example, `radius` is a `Double`, `numOfColumns` is an `Int`, while `myName` is a `String`. How can the programmer verify the variable type? A good way is to use Xcode's Playground feature. Go ahead and type the preceding statements into your Playground project. Then, Option-click on each of the constants and look at the pop-up that appears. Figure 1-13 shows that the type of `radius` is `Double`.

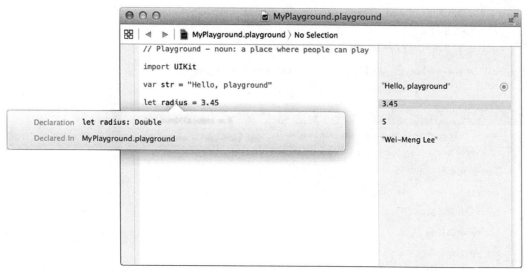

FIGURE 1-13

Readers familiar with Objective-C will immediately note the lack of the @ character when defining a string literal. In Objective-C, you need the @ character before a string:

```
NSString *myName = @"Wei-Meng Lee"     //---Objective-C---
```

However, it is not needed in Swift:

```
let myName = "Wei-Meng Lee"            //---Swift---
```

Also, in Objective-C you need to use the * to indicate memory pointers whenever you are dealing with objects; in Swift there is no need to use the *, regardless of whether you are using objects or primitive types.

> **NOTE** Strictly speaking, the String type in Swift is a primitive (value) type, whereas the NSString in Objective-C is a reference type (object). Strings are discussed in more detail in Chapter 3.

If you wish to declare the type of constant, you can do so using the colon operator (:) followed by the data type, as shown here:

```
let diameter:Double = 8
```

The preceding statement declares diameter to be a Double constant. You want to declare it explicitly because you are assigning an integer value to it. If you don't do this, the compiler will assume it is an integer constant.

Once a constant is created, you can no longer change its value:

```
let radius = 3.45
radius = 5.67    //---error---
```

Figure 1-14 shows Playground flagging the statement as an error.

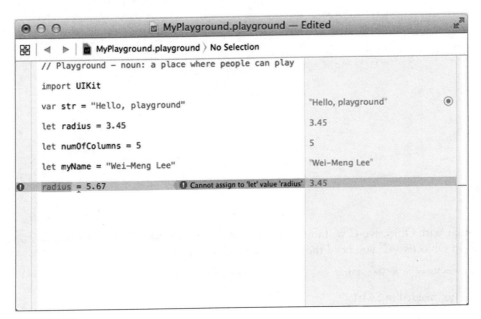

FIGURE 1-14

Variables

To declare a variable, you use the var keyword:

```
let radius = 3.45
var myAge = 25
var circumference = 2 * 3.14 * radius
```

Once a variable is created, you can change its value:

```
let diameter = 20.5
circumference = 2 * 3.14 * diameter/2
```

Observe that after you type the preceding statements into Playground, the value of circumference is immediately computed and the result shown on the right (see Figure 1-15).

In Swift, values are never implicitly converted to another type. For example, suppose you are trying to concatenate a string and the value of a variable. In the following example, you need to explicitly use the String() initializer to convert the value of myAge to a string value before concatenating it with another string:

```
var strMyAge = "My age is " + String(myAge)
//---My age is 25---
```

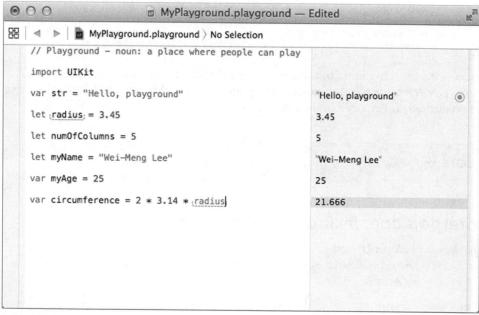

FIGURE 1-15

If you type the preceding statements into Playground, the value of `strMyAge` is immediately shown on the right (see Figure 1-16).

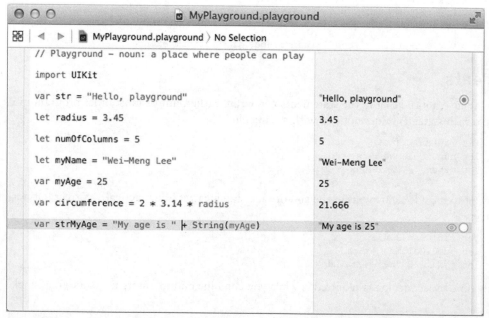

FIGURE 1-16

Interestingly, an error will occur if you try to do something such as the following:

```
var strCircumference =
    "Circumference of circle is " +  String(circumference)
```

This is because the `String()` initializer cannot convert the `Double` type (the `circumference` variable by type inference is `Double`) into a `String` type. To solve this, you need to use the string interpolation method, as described in the next section.

> **NOTE** *You will learn more about data types in the next chapter.*

String Interpolation: Including Values in Strings

One of the dreaded tasks in Objective-C is inserting values of variables in a string. (You have to use the `NSString` class and its associated `stringWithFormat:` method to perform string concatenation, which makes your code really long.)

In Swift, this is very easy using the `\()` syntax, known as *string interpolation*. It has the following format:

```
"Your string literal \(variable_name)"
```

The following example shows how:

```
let myName = "Wei-Meng Lee"
var strName = "My name is \(myName)"
```

You can use this method to include a `Double` value in your string as shown here:

```
var strResult = "The circumference is \(circumference)"
```

Statements

You might have noticed that in the statements you wrote earlier, unlike most other programming languages each statement does not end with a semicolon (`;`):

```
let radius = 3.45
let numOfColumns = 5
let myName = "Wei-Meng Lee"
```

If you want to include semicolons at the end of each statement, it is syntactically correct but not necessary:

```
let radius = 3.45;
let numOfColumns = 5;
let myName = "Wei-Meng Lee";
```

The only time the semicolon is required is when you combine multiple statements into one single line:

```
let radius = 3.45; let numOfColumns = 5; let myName = "Wei-Meng Lee";
```

Printing

You can print the current values of variables or constants using the `println()` or `print()` function. The `print()` function prints out the value, whereas the `println()` function does the same and additionally prints a line break. These two functions are similar to Cocoa's `NSLog` function (for readers who are familiar with Objective-C).

In Playground, the `println()` and `print()` functions print the values to the Console Output window in the Timeline; in Xcode, these functions print out the values to the Output window. The following statements print out the value of `strMyAge`:

```
var strMyAge = "My age is " + String(myAge)
println(strMyAge)
```

Figure 1-17 shows the output of the preceding statements in Xcode's Output window. (Press Command+Shift+C to reveal the Output window.)

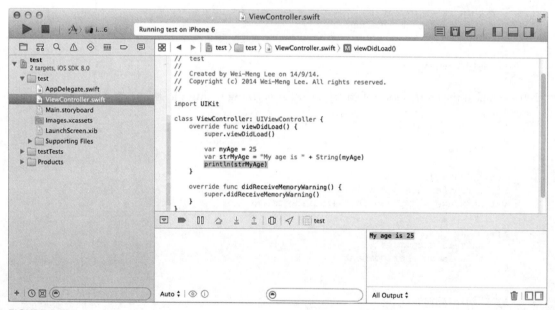

FIGURE 1-17

Comments

In Swift, as in most programming languages, you insert comments into your code using two forward slashes (//):

```
// this is a comment
// this is another comment
```

The // characters mark the line as a comment. The compiler ignores comments at compilation time.

If you have several lines of comments, it is better to use the /* and */ combination to denote a block of statements as comments. For example:

```
/*
    this is a comment
    this is another comment
*/
```

The two preceding lines are marked as a comment.

You can also nest comments, as shown in the following example:

```
// this is a comment

var myAge = 25
var circumference = 2 * 3.14 * radius
var strMyAge = "My age is " + String(myAge)

/*
    this is a comment
    this is another comment
*/

println(strMyAge)
```

To comment the entire block of code, enclose everything within the /* and */, as shown here:

```
/*

// this is a comment

var myAge = 25
var circumference = 2 * 3.14 * radius
var strMyAge = "My age is " + String(myAge)

/*
    this is a comment
    this is another comment
*/

println(strMyAge)

*/
```

> **NOTE** *In other languages such as C and Java, you are not allowed to nest comments.*

SUMMARY

In this chapter, you learned about Apple's motives for creating Swift, as well as how to obtain the tools to start learning it. You also had a brief look at its syntax. If you have been an Objective-C developer until now, your first impression of Swift is likely a positive one, as it is a thoroughly contemporary and safe language, without the obscure syntax of Objective-C. In the following chapters, you will learn about various other impressive aspects of Swift.

EXERCISES

1. Declare three constants: to store the number of months in a year, the number of days in a week, and the number of weeks in a year.

2. Declare variables to store a user's gender, weight, height, and date of birth.

3. Write statement(s) to print out the details of the user using the variables that you have declared in question #2.

4. The following statements resulted in a compiler error. Fix it.

```
var weight = 102.5       // in pounds
var str = "Your weight is " + weight + " pounds"
```

▶ **WHAT YOU LEARNED IN THIS CHAPTER**

TOPIC	KEY CONCEPTS
Declaring constants	You declare a constant using the `let` keyword.
Declaring variables	You declare a variable using the `var` keyword.
Printing values of constants or variables	You can use the `print()` or `println()` functions to print out the values of variables or constants.
No need for semicolons	Each statement in Swift does *not* need to end with a semicolon. However, a semicolon(s) is needed if you are combining multiple statements into a single line.
Including the value of variables or constants in strings	The easiest way to include these values is to use the string interpolation method: `"\()"`
Comments	You can use `//` to comment a single line, or use the `/*` and `*/` combination to comment out a block of statements. In Swift, comments can be nested.

2

Data Types

WHAT YOU WILL LEARN IN THIS CHAPTER:

➤ The basic data types: integers, floating-point numbers, and Booleans

➤ The types of integers

➤ How to perform integer operations

➤ Different ways to represent integer literals

➤ The two different floating-point types

➤ How to perform floating-point operations

➤ Different ways to represent floating-point literals

➤ How to create type aliases

➤ What tuples are

➤ The new optional types

➤ How to declare implicitly unwrapped optionals

➤ How to perform optional binding

➤ How to unwrap optionals using the ? character

➤ How to define enumerations

In Chapter 1, you took a quick look at the syntax of Swift statements, as well as how to declare variables and constants quickly using type inference. In this chapter, you will learn more about the various data types available in the language.

In addition to supporting the various basic data types available in most programming languages, Swift also introduces new data types not available in Objective-C. Such new data types include the following:

➤ **Tuples**—A tuple is a group of related values that can be manipulated as a single data type. Tuples are very useful when you need to return multiple values from a function.

➤ **Optional types**—An optional type specifies a variable that can contain no value. Optional types make your code safer, as you will learn later in this chapter.

Swift is a type-safe language. In most cases, you have to perform explicit type conversions when assigning values from one type to another. Also, variables that are not assigned a value are not allowed to be used in a statement and will be flagged as errors.

BASIC DATA TYPES

Like most programming languages, Swift provides the following basic data types:

➤ Integers

➤ Floating-point numbers

➤ Booleans

Integers

Integers are whole numbers with no fractional parts. Integers can be positive or negative. In Swift, integers are represented using the Int type. The Int type represents both positive as well as negative values. If you only need to store positive values, you can use the unsigned integer UInt type. The size of an Int type depends on the system on which your code is running. On 32-bit systems, Int and UInt each use 32 bits for storage, whereas on 64-bit systems Int and UInt each use 64 bits.

You can programmatically check the number of bytes stored by each data type using the sizeof() function:

```
println("Size of Int: \(sizeof(Int)) bytes")
println("Size of UInt: \(sizeof(UInt)) bytes")
```

If you run the preceding statement on an iPhone 5 (which uses the 32-bit A6 chip), you will get the following:

```
Size of Int: 4 bytes
Size of UInt: 4 bytes
```

If you run the preceding statement on an iPhone 5s (which uses the 64-bit A7 chip), you will get the following:

```
Size of Int: 8 bytes
Size of UInt: 8 bytes
```

If you do not know the type of data a variable is storing, you can use the `sizeofValue()` function:

```
var num = 5
println("Size of num: \(sizeofValue(num)) bytes")
```

Types of Integers

In most cases, you will use `Int` for storing signed numbers, and `UInt` if you do not need to store negative values (even if you don't need to store negative numbers it is still a good idea to use `Int` for code compatibility). However, if you want to explicitly control the size of the variable used, you can specify one of the various integer types available:

➤ `Int8` and `UInt8`

➤ `Int16` and `UInt16`

➤ `Int32` and `UInt32`

➤ `Int64` and `UInt64`

> **NOTE** On 32-bit systems, `Int` is the same as `Int32`, while on 64-bit systems, `Int` is the same as `Int64`.
>
> On 32-bit systems, `UInt` is the same as `UInt32`, while on 64-bit systems, `UInt` is the same as `UInt64`.

The following code snippet prints the range of numbers representable for each integer type:

```
//---UInt8  - Min: 0 Max: 255---
println("UInt8  - Min: \(UInt8.min) Max: \(UInt8.max)")

//---UInt16 - Min: 0 Max: 65535---
println("UInt16 - Min: \(UInt16.min) Max: \(UInt16.max)")

//---UInt32 - Min: 0 Max: 4294967295---
println("UInt32 - Min: \(UInt32.min) Max: \(UInt32.max)")

//---UInt64 - Min: 0 Max: 18446744073709551615---
println("UInt64 - Min: \(UInt64.min) Max: \(UInt64.max)")

//---Int8  - Min: -128 Max: 127---
println("Int8   - Min: \(Int8.min) Max: \(Int8.max)")
```

```
//---Int16 - Min: -32768 Max: 32767---
println("Int16 - Min: \(Int16.min) Max: \(Int16.max)")

//---Int32 - Min: -2147483648 Max: 2147483647---
println("Int32 - Min: \(Int32.min) Max: \(Int32.max)")

//---Int64 - Min: -9223372036854775808 Max: 9223372036854775807---
println("Int64 - Min: \(Int64.min) Max: \(Int64.max)")
```

For each integer type, the min property returns the minimum number representable and the max property returns the maximum number representable.

Integer Operations

When you try to add two numbers of different integer types, you will get an error. Consider the following example:

```
var i1: UInt8 = 255
var i2: UInt16 = 255
var i3 = i1 + i2      //---cannot add two variables of different types---
```

To fix this, you need to typecast one of the types to be the same as the other type:

```
var i3 = UInt16(i1) + i2  //---i3 is now UInt16---
```

Integer Literals

You can represent integer values as follows:

➤ Decimal

➤ Binary—Use the 0b prefix.

➤ Octal—Use the 0o prefix.

➤ Hexadecimal—Use the 0x prefix.

The following code snippet shows the number 15 represented in the four forms:

```
let num1 = 15        //---decimal---
let num2 = 0b1111    //---binary
let num3 = 0o17      //---octal---
let num4 = 0xF       //---hexadecimal---
```

You can pad the integers with zeros if you want to make them more readable. The preceding code snippet can be rewritten as the following statements without changing the value represented:

```
let num1 = 00000015    //---decimal---
let num2 = 0b001111    //---binary
let num3 = 0o000017    //---octal---
let num4 = 0x00000F    //---hexadecimal---
```

In addition, for big numbers, you can also use underscores (_) to make them more readable. For example, instead of writing one billion as:

```
let billion = 1000000000
```

you can use the underscore to make it more readable:

```
let billion = 1_000_000_000
```

The placement of the underscore is not important; the following represents the same value as the previous statement:

```
let billion = 100_00_00_00_0
```

Floating-Point Numbers

Floating-point numbers are numbers with fractional parts. Examples of floating-point numbers are 0.0123, 2.45, and −4.521. In Swift, there are two floating-point types: `Float` and `Double`. `Float` uses 32 bits for storage and `Double` uses 64 bits. This can be confirmed using the `sizeof()` function:

```
println("Size of Double: \(sizeof(Double)) bytes")
println("Size of Float: \(sizeof(Float)) bytes")
```

`Double` has a precision of at least 15 decimal digits, while `Float` has a precision of at least six decimal digits.

When assigning a floating-point number to a constant or variable, Swift will always infer the `Double` type unless you explicitly specify otherwise:

```
var num1 = 3.14         //---num1 is Double---
var num2: Float = 3.14  //---num2 is Float---
```

If you try to assign a `Double` to a `Float` type, the compiler will flag an error:

```
num2 = num1      //---num1 is Double and num2 is Float---
```

This is because the number stored in a `Double` type may not be able to fit into a `Float` type, thereby resulting in an overflow. In order to assign `num1` to `num2`, you need to explicitly cast `num1` to a `Float`, like this:

```
num2 = Float(num1)
```

Floating-Point Operations

When you add an integer constant to a `Double`, the resultant type would also be a `Double` type. Likewise, when you add an integer constant to a `Float`, the resultant type would also be a `Float` type, as the following example illustrates:

```
var sum1 = 5 + num1   //---num1 and sum1 are both Double---
var sum2 = 5 + num2   //---num2 and sum2 are both Float---
```

However, if you try to add `Int` and `Double` variables, you will get an error:

```
var i4: Int = 123
var f1: Double = 3.14567
var r = i4 + f1          //---error---
```

In order to add two variables of different types, you need to cast the `Int` variable to `Double`:

```
var r = Double(i4) + f1
```

When you add an integer to a floating-point number, the result would be a `Double` value. For example:

```
var someNumber = 5 + 3.14
```

In the preceding statement, `someNumber` would be inferred to be a `Double`.

In Swift, for safety reasons there is no implicit type conversion—you must explicitly convert an `Int` to a `Float` (or `Double`):

```
var f:Float
var i:Int = 5
f = i  //---error---
f = Float(i)
```

When you cast a floating-point value to an integer, the value is always truncated—that is, you will lose its fractional part:

```
var floatNum = 3.5
var intNum = Int(floatNum)  //---intNum is now 3---
```

Floating-Point Literals

You can represent floating-point values as follows:

➤   Decimal

➤   Hexadecimal—Use the `0x` prefix

The following code snippet shows the floating-point number 345.678 represented in the two forms:

```
let num5 = 345.678
let num6 = 3.45678E2    // 3.45678 x 10^2
let num7 = 34567.8E-2   // 3.45678 x 10^(-2)
```

The `E` (it can also be written as the lowercase "e") represents the exponent. `3.45678E2` means 3.45678 times 10 to the power of two.

You can also represent a hexadecimal floating-point number with an exponent of base 2:

```
let num8 = 0x2Cp3    // 44 x 2^3
let num9 = 0x2Cp-3   // 44 x 2^(-3)
```

In this case, `2Cp3` means `2C` (hexadecimal; which is 44 in decimal) times two to the power of three.

Type Alias

A type alias enables you to define an alternative name for the existing data type. For example, using the built-in types you can specify the data type for variables like this:

```
var customerID: UInt32
var customerName: String
```

However, it would be more useful if you could provide a more meaningful and contextually relevant name using the `typealias` keyword:

```
typealias CustomerIDType = UInt32
typealias CustomerNameType = String
```

In the preceding code snippet, `CustomerIDType` is now the alias for the `UInt32` type, and `CustomerNameType` is the alias for the `String` type. You can use the aliases as if they are the data types, like this:

```
var customerID: CustomerIDType
var customerName: CustomerNameType

customerID = 12345
customerName = "Chloe Lee"
```

Boolean

Swift supports the Boolean logic type—`Bool`. A `Bool` type can take either a `true` or `false` value.

> **NOTE** Unlike Objective-C, in which a Boolean value can be YES or NO, the `Bool` values in Swift are similar to most programming languages like Java and C. It does not support Objective-C's YES or NO value.

The following code snippet shows the `Bool` type in use:

```
var skyIsBlue = true
var seaIsGreen = false
var areYouKidding:Bool = true

skyIsBlue = !true    //---skyIsBlue is now false---
println(skyIsBlue)   //---false---
```

`Bool` variables are often used in conditional statements such as the If statement:

```
if areYouKidding {
    println("Just joking, huh?")
} else {
    println("Are you serious?")
}
```

> **NOTE** *Chapter 7 discusses the If statement in more detail.*

TUPLES

A tuple is an ordered collection of values. The values inside a tuple can be of any type; they need not be all of the same type. Consider the example in which you want to store the coordinates of a point in the coordinate space:

```
var x = 7
var y = 8
```

This used two variables to store the *x* and *y* coordinates of a point. Because these two values are related, it is much better to store them together as a tuple instead of two individual integer variables, as shown here:

```
var pt = (7,8)
```

In the preceding statement, pt is a tuple containing two values: 7 and 8. You can also rewrite the tuple as follows:

```
var pt: (Int, Int)
pt = (7,8)
```

In this case, it is now obvious that the pt is a tuple of type (Int, Int).

Here are some more examples of tuples:

```
var flight = (7031, "ATL", "ORD")
//---tuple of type (Int, String, String)---

var phone = ("Chloe", "732-757-2923")
//---tuple of type (String, String)---
```

If you want to retrieve the individual values inside a tuple, you can assign it to individual variables or constants:

```
var flight = (7031, "ATL", "ORD")
let (flightno, orig, dest) = flight
println(flightno)   //---7031---
println(orig)       //---ATL---
println(dest)       //---ORD---
```

If you are not interested in some values within the tuple, use the underscore (_) character in place of variables or constants:

```
let (flightno, _, _) = flight
println(flightno)
```

Alternatively, you can also access the individual values inside the tuple using the index, starting from 0:

```
println(flight.0)   //---7031---
println(flight.1)   //---ATL---
println(flight.2)   //---ORD---
```

Using the index to access the individual values inside a tuple is not intuitive. A better way is to name the individual elements inside the tuple:

```
var flight = (flightno:7031, orig:"ATL", dest:"ORD")
```

Once the individual elements are named, you can access them using those names:

```
println(flight.flightno)
println(flight.orig)
println(flight.dest)
```

> **NOTE** One common use for a tuple is returning multiple values in a function. Chapter 5 discusses this topic in more detail.

OPTIONAL TYPES

Swift uses a new concept known as *optionals*. To understand this concept, consider the following code snippet:

```
let str = "125"
let num = str.toInt()
```

Here, `str` is a string, and the `String` type has a method named `toInt()` that converts a `String` to an integer. However, the conversion may not always be successful (the string may contain characters that cannot be converted to a number) and the result returned to `num` may be an `Int` value or `nil`. Hence, by type inference, `num` is assigned a type of `Int?`.

The `?` character indicates that this variable can *optionally* contain a value—it might not contain a value at all if the conversion is not successful (in which case `num` will be assigned a `nil` value). In the preceding code snippet, any attempt to use the `num` variable (such as multiplying it with another variable/constant) will result in a compiler error—"value of optional type 'Int?' not unwrapped; did you mean to use '!' or '?'?":

```
let multiply = num * 2   //---error---
```

To fix this, you should use the If statement to determine whether `num` does indeed contain a value. If it does, you need to use the `!` character after the variable name to use its value, like this:

```
let str = "125"
let num = str.toInt()
```

```
if num != nil {
    let multiply = num! * 2
    println(multiply)    //---250---
}
```

The ! character indicates to the compiler that you know that the variable contains a value and you indeed know what you are doing.

> **NOTE** *The use of the* ! *character is known as* forced unwrapping of an optional's value.

In the previous example, num is an optional due to type inference. If you want to explicitly declare a variable as an optional type, you can append the ? character to the type name. For example, the following statement declares description to be an optional string type:

```
var description: String?
```

You can assign a string to description:

```
description = "Hello"
```

You can also assign the special value nil to an optional type:

```
description = nil
```

> **NOTE** *You cannot assign* nil *to a non-optional type.*

Implicitly Unwrapped Optionals

In the previous section you saw the use of the optional type and the use of the ! character to unwrap the value of an optional variable. The problem with this is that you likely will end up with a lot of ! characters in your code whenever you access the value of the optional variable. To access the value of an optional variable without using the ! character, you can declare an optional type as an *implicitly unwrapped optional.*

Consider the following declaration:

```
//---implicit optional variable---
var str2: String! = "This is a string"
```

Here, str2 is an implicitly unwrapped optional. When you access str2, there is no need to use the ! character, as it is implicitly unwrapped:

```
println(str2) // "This is a string"
```

If str2 is set to nil, accessing the str2 will return a nil:

```
str2 = nil
println(str2) // nil
```

Optional Binding

Many times you need to assign the value of an optional type to another variable or constant. Consider the following example:

```
var productCode:String? = getProductCode("Diet Coke")
if let tempProductCode = productCode {
    println(tempProductCode)
} else {
    println("Product Code not found")
}
```

In this snippet, getProductCode() is a function that takes in a product name (of String type) and returns a product code (a String value) or nil if the product cannot be found. As such, the productCode is an optional String.

To assign the value of productCode to another variable/constant, you can use the following pattern:

```
if let tempProductCode = productCode {
```

Here, you are essentially doing this: check the value of productCode; if it is not nil, assign the value to tempProductCode and execute the If block of statements—otherwise, execute the Else block of statements.

You can easily test this by setting productCode to a value:

```
productCode = "12345"
if let tempProductCode = productCode {
    println(tempProductCode)
} else {
    println("Product Code not found")
}
```

The preceding code snippet will print out:

```
12345
```

If you now set productCode to nil:

```
productCode = nil
if let tempProductCode = productCode {
    println(tempProductCode)
} else {
    println("Product Code not found")
}
```

The preceding code snippet will print out:

```
Product Code not found
```

Unwrapping Optionals Using "?"

So far you have learned that you can use the ! character to unwrap an optional type's value. Consider the following scenario:

```
var str:String?
var empty = str!.isEmpty
```

From this code snippet, str is an optional String and isEmpty is a property from the String class. In this example, you want to know if str is empty, so you call the isEmpty property. However, the preceding code will crash, as str contains nil, and trying to call the isEmpty property from nil results in a runtime error. The use of the ! character is like telling the compiler: I am very confident that str is not nil, so please go ahead and call the isEmpty property. Unfortunately, str is indeed nil in this case.

To prevent the statement from crashing, you should instead use the ? character, as follows:

```
var empty = str?.isEmpty
```

The ? character tells the compiler: I am not sure if str is nil. If it is not nil, please call the isEmpty property; otherwise, ignore it.

ENUMERATIONS

An enumeration is a user-defined type consisting of a group of named constants. The best way to explain an enumeration is to use an example. Suppose you want to create a variable to store the color of a bag. You can store the color as a string, like this:

```
var colorOfBag = "Black"
```

The color can also be changed to, for example, "Yellow":

```
colorOfBag = "Yellow"
```

However, using this approach is not safe, as there are two potential pitfalls:

➤   The color may be set to a color that is invalid—for example, a bag's color can only be Black or Green. If the color is set to Yellow, your code will not be able to detect it.

➤   The color specified might not be the same case you expected. If your code expected "Black" and you assigned "black" to the variable, your code might break.

In either case, it is always better to be able to define your own type to represent all the different colors that a bag may be. In this case, you create an *enumeration* containing all the valid colors. The following code snippet defines an enumeration named BagColor:

```
enum BagColor {
    case Black
    case White
    case Red
    case Green
    case Yellow
}
```

The `BagColor` enumeration contains five cases (also known as members): `Black`, `White`, `Red`, `Green`, and `Yellow`. Each member is declared using the `case` keyword. You can also group the five separate cases into one single case, separated using commas (,), as shown here:

```
enum BagColor {
    case Black, White, Red, Green, Yellow
}
```

You can now declare a variable of this enumeration type:

```
var colorOfBag:BagColor
```

To assign a value to this variable, specify the enumeration name, followed by its member:

```
colorOfBag = BagColor.Yellow
```

> **NOTE** *In Swift, you need to specify the enumeration name followed by its member. This is different from Objective-C, for which you just need to specify the member name, e.g.,* `UITableViewCellAccessoryDetailDisclosureButton`. *The approach in Swift makes the code more comprehensible.*

You can omit the enumeration name by simply specifying its member name:

```
colorOfBag = .Yellow
```

Using Enumeration in Switch Statements

Enumerations are often used in Switch statements. The following code snippet checks the value of `colorOfBag` and outputs the respective statement:

```
switch colorOfBag {
    case BagColor.Black:
        println("Black")
    case BagColor.White:
        println("White")
    case BagColor.Red:
        println("Red")
    case BagColor.Green:
        println("Green")
    case BagColor.Yellow:
        println("Yellow")
}
```

Because the type of colorOfBag (which is BagColor) is already known, Swift allows you to specify only the enumeration members and omit the name:

```
switch colorOfBag {
    case .Black:
        println("Black")
    case .White:
        println("White")
    case .Red:
        println("Red")
    case .Green:
        println("Green")
    case .Yellow:
        println("Yellow")
}
```

Enumeration Raw Values

One of the common operations that you need to perform with enumerations is that of associating a value with the members of an enumeration. For example, suppose you want to store the value of colorOfBag to a file as a string (or, if you like, an integer). In this case, Swift makes it very easy for you to associate a value to members of an enumeration:

```
enum BagColor: String {
    case Black = "Black"
    case White  = "White"
    case Red = "Red"
    case Green = "Green"
    case Yellow = "Yellow"
}
```

After the declaration of the enumeration, append the enumeration name with a colon (:) and indicate the type of data to which you want each member associated (all members must be of the same type):

```
enum BagColor: String {
```

> **NOTE** The String *in the preceding code snippet is known as the* raw type.

Within the enumeration, you then assign each member to the desired value, of the type that you have just specified:

```
    case Black = "Black"
    case White  = "White"
    case Red = "Red"
    case Green = "Green"
    case Yellow = "Yellow"
```

To obtain the value of an enumeration, use the `rawValue` property of the enumeration instance:

```
var colorOfBag:BagColor
colorOfBag = BagColor.Yellow
var c = colorOfBag.rawValue
println(c)   //---prints out "Yellow"---
```

The `rawValue` property will return the value that you have assigned to each member of the enumeration.

What about the reverse? If you have a string of `"Green"`, how do you convert it to the enumeration member? You can do so via the `rawValue` initializer, as follows:

```
var colorOfSecondBag:BagColor? = BagColor(rawValue:"Green")
```

The preceding statement uses the `rawValue` initializer to try to convert the string `"Green"` to the enumeration member from `BagColor`. Because the `rawValue` initializer does not guarantee that it is able to return an enumeration member (imagine you pass in a value of, for example, `"Brown"`), it returns an optional value—hence, the `?` sign in the statement. Once the value is returned, you can proceed to use it:

```
if colorOfSecondBag == BagColor.Green {
    . . .
}
```

If you want to use the `rawValue` property on `colorOfSecondBag`, you should confirm that it is not `nil` before proceeding to use it:

```
//---print only if colorOfSecondBag is not nil---
if colorOfSecondBag != nil {
    println(colorOfSecondBag!.rawValue)
}
```

You also need to have a `!` character to force unwrap the value of `colorOfSecondBag` before accessing the `rawValue` property.

Auto-Increment for Raw Values

In the previous section you saw that you could assign string values to each member in an enumeration. Very often, you would also assign integer values instead of strings. A good example is when you are representing the day of a week, as shown in the following code snippet:

```
enum DayOfWeek: Int {
    case Monday = 1
    case Tuesday = 2
```

```
    case Wednesday = 3
    case Thursday = 4
    case Friday = 5
    case Saturday = 6
    case Sunday = 7
}
```

From the preceding statements, you can see that each day of the week is assigned an integer value—Monday is assigned 1, Tuesday is assigned 2, and so on. The following statements show how it can be used:

```
var d = DayOfWeek.Wednesday
println(d.rawValue)    //---prints out 3---
```

When integer values are used for raw values within an enumeration, they are automatically incremented if no values are specified for subsequent members. For example, the following code snippet shows that only the first member within the DayOfWeek enumeration is set to a value:

```
enum DayOfWeek: Int {
    case Monday = 1
    case Tuesday
    case Wednesday
    case Thursday
    case Friday
    case Saturday
    case Sunday
}
```

Due to auto-incrementing of integer raw values, the following will still work:

```
var d = DayOfWeek.Thursday
println(d.rawValue)    //---prints out 4---
```

Associated Values

The previous section demonstrated how you can assign a value to each member of an enumeration. Sometimes, it would be very useful to be able to store a particular value (or values) associated with a particular member of an enumeration. Consider the following code snippets:

```
enum NetworkType: String {
    case LTE = "LTE"
    case ThreeG = "3G"
}

enum DeviceType {
    case Phone (NetworkType, String)
    case Tablet(String)
}
```

The first enumeration, NetworkType, represents the type of network to which a phone can connect. The second enumeration, DeviceType, represents two types of devices: Phone or Tablet. If a device is a phone, you would want to store some values associated with it—in this case, you want to store its network type and the model of the device. If a device is a tablet, you would just store the model of the device.

To use the preceding enumerations declared, take a look at the following code snippet:

```
var device1 = DeviceType.Phone(NetworkType.LTE, "iPhone 5S")
var device2 = DeviceType.Tablet("iPad Air")
```

For `device1`, its type is a phone and you store the associated information (network type and model name) with it. For `device2`, its type is a tablet and you store its model name with it.

You can use a Switch statement to extract the associated value of an enumeration:

```
switch device1 {
    case .Phone(let networkType, let model):
        println("\(networkType.rawValue) - \(model)")
    case .Tablet(let model):
        println("\(model)")
}
```

The preceding code snippet will output the following line:

```
LTE - iPhone 5S
```

Enumeration Functions

You can define a function within an enumeration. Using the same example used in the previous section, we'll now add a function named `info` to the `DeviceType` enumeration:

```
enum DeviceType {
    case Phone (NetworkType, String)
    case Tablet(String)
    var info: String {
        switch (self) {
            case let .Phone (networkType, model):
                return "\(networkType.rawValue) - \(model)"
            case let .Tablet (model):
                return "\(model)"
        }
    }
}
```

In the preceding code snippet, the `info()` function returns a string. It checks the member that is currently selected (using the `self` keyword) and returns either a string containing the network type and model (for phone) or simply the model (for tablet). To use the function, simply call it with the enumeration instance, as shown here:

```
println(device1.info)   //---LTE - iPhone 5S---
println(device2.info)   //---iPad Air---
```

SUMMARY

In this chapter, you had a more detailed look at the basic data types supported by Swift. In addition, you also learned about some of the features that make Swift a type-safe language. In addition, Swift also introduces some new features, such as optional types, as well as tuples. Enumerations in Swift have also been greatly enhanced with the support for raw values, associated values, as well as internal functions.

EXERCISES

1. Consider the following code snippet. The compiler generates an error. Suggest ways to fix it.

```
var weightInPounds = 154
var heightInInches = 66.9
var BMI = (weightInPounds / pow(heightInInches,2)) * 703.06957964
println(BMI)
```

2. Examine the following code snippet:

```
enum cartoonCharacters: Int {
    case FelixTheCat = 1
    case AngelicaPickles
    case ThePowerpuffGirls
    case SpiderMan = 9
    case GeorgeOfTheJungle
    case Superman
    case Batman
}
```

What is the output for the following statements?

```
var d = cartoonCharacters.GeorgeOfTheJungle
println(d.rawValue)

d = cartoonCharacters.AngelicaPickles
println(d.rawValue)
```

3. Examine the following code snippet:

```
enum cartoonCharacters: Int {
    case FelixTheCat
    case AngelicaPickles
    case ThePowerpuffGirls
    case SpiderMan = 9
    case GeorgeOfTheJungle
    case Superman
    case Batman
}
```

What is the output for the following statements?

```
var d = cartoonCharacters.GeorgeOfTheJungle
println(d.rawValue)

d = cartoonCharacters.AngelicaPickles
println(d.rawValue)
```

4. The following code snippets cause the compiler to generate an error. Fix it.

```
var isMember:Bool?
if isMember {
    println("User is a member")
} else {
    println("User is a not member")
}
```

▶ **WHAT YOU LEARNED IN THIS CHAPTER**

TOPIC	KEY CONCEPTS
Integers	Integers are represented using the `Int` and `UInt` types. You can also use specific-sized types, such as `Int8` and `UInt8`, `Int16` and `UInt16`, `Int32` and `UInt32`, or `Int64` and `UInt64`.
Integers representations	Integers can be represented as decimal, binary, octal, or hexadecimal.
Floating-point numbers	Floating-point numbers are represented using the `Float` or `Double` type.
Floating-point numbers representations	Floating-point numbers can be represented as decimal or hexadecimal.
Boolean values	A Boolean value is either `true` or `false`.
Tuples	A tuple is an order collection of values.
Optional types	An optional type variable can either contain a value or `nil`.
Unwrapping optional variables	To unwrap the value of an optional variable, use the `!` character.
Implicitly unwrapped optionals	If you declare a type to be an implicitly unwrapped optional, there is no need to use the `!` character to unwrap the type.
Optional binding	Optional binding allows a value of an optional to be assigned to another variable directly.
Unwrapping an optional using `?`	If you are not sure if an optional variable is `nil` or not before calling its methods or properties, use the `?` character
Enumerations	An enumeration is a user-defined type consisting of a group of named constants.
Enumeration raw values	You can assign a value to each member of an enumeration.
Enumeration auto-increment values	You can assign an integer value to a member of an enumeration; the compiler will automatically increment the value and assign them to each subsequent members.
Enumeration associated value	You can store a value to associate with a particular member of an enumeration.
Enumeration functions	An enumeration can also contain a function within its definition.

3

Strings and Characters

WHAT YOU WILL LEARN IN THIS CHAPTER:

➤ How to define a string literal

➤ The copy behavior of strings

➤ The difference between characters and strings

➤ How to use the various special string characters

➤ How to use Unicode characters in Swift

➤ How to use the various common string functions

➤ How type conversion works for strings

➤ How the `String` type interoperates with the `NSString` class

In the previous chapter, you learned about the various basic data types supported in Swift as well as some of the new features it introduces—tuples, optional types, and enhanced enumerations. In this chapter, you will learn how strings are represented in Swift using the `String` type and how it is bridged seamlessly with the `NSString` class found in the Foundation framework in Objective-C. In particular, because Swift supports Unicode natively, there are some areas that you need to pay attention to when dealing with strings. All of these are discussed in this chapter.

STRINGS

In Swift, a string literal is a sequence of characters enclosed by a pair of double quotes (""). The following code snippet shows a string literal assigned to a constant and another to a variable:

```
let str1 = "This is a string in Swift"        //---str1 is a constant---
var str2 = "This is another string in Swift"  //---str2 is a variable---
```

Because the compiler uses type inference, there is no need to specify the type of constant and variable that is being assigned the string. However, if you wish, you could still specify the String type explicitly:

```
var str3:String = "This is yet another string in Swift"
```

To assign an empty string to a variable, you can simply use a pair of empty double quotes, or call the initializer of the String type, like this:

```
var str4 = ""
var str5 = String()
```

The preceding statements initialize both str4 and str5 to contain an empty string. To check whether a variable contains an empty string, use the isEmpty() method of the String type:

```
if str4.isEmpty {
    println("Empty string")
}
```

Mutability of Strings

The *mutability* of a string means whether it can be modified after it has been assigned to a variable. In Swift, a string's mutability is dependent on whether it is assigned to a constant or a variable.

A string that is assigned to a variable is mutable, as the following shows:

```
var myName = "Wei-Meng"
myName += " Lee"
println(myName)  //---Wei-Meng Lee---
```

A string that is assigned to a constant is *immutable* (i.e., not mutable—its value cannot be changed):

```
let yourName = "Joe"
yourName += "Sim"     //---error---
yourName = "James"    //---error---
```

Strings as Value Types

In Swift, String is a value type. This means that when you assign a string to another variable, or pass a string into a function, a copy of the string is always created. Consider the following code snippet:

```
var originalStr = "This is the original"
var copyStr = originalStr
```

In the preceding example, `originalStr` is initialized with a string literal and then assigned to `copyStr`. A copy of the string literal is copied and assigned to `copyStr`, as shown in Figure 3-1.

FIGURE 3-1

If you output the values of both variables, you can see that both output the same string literal:

```
println(originalStr)    //---This is the original---
println(copyStr)        //---This is the original---
```

Now let's make a change to the `copyStr` variable by assigning it another string literal:

```
copyStr = "This is the copy!"
```

What happened here is that `copyStr` is now assigned another string, as shown in Figure 3-2.

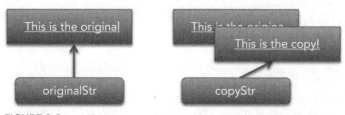

FIGURE 3-2

To prove this, output the values of both variables:

```
println(originalStr)
println(copyStr)
```

The preceding code snippet would output the following:

```
This is the original
This is the copy!
```

Characters

As mentioned earlier, in Swift a string is made up of *characters*. You can iterate through a string and extract each character using the For-In loop. The following code snippet shows an example:

```
var helloWorld = "Hello, World!"
```

```
for c in helloWorld {
    println(c)
}
```

The preceding statements output the following:

```
H
e
l
l
o
,

W
o
r
l
d
!
```

The For-In loop works with Unicode characters as well:

```
var hello = "您好"  //---hello contains two Chinese characters---
for c in hello {
    println(c)
}
```

The preceding code snippet outputs the following:

```
您
好
```

By default, using type inference the compiler will always use the `String` type for a character enclosed with double quotes. For example, in the following statement, euro is inferred to be of `String` type:

```
var euro = "€"
```

However, if you want euro to be the `Character` type, you have to explicitly specify the `Character` type:

```
var euro:Character = "€"
```

To append a string to a character, you need to convert the character to a string, as the following shows:

```
var euro:Character = "€"
var price = String(euro) + "2500"  //---€2500---
euro += "2500"                     //---error---
```

Concatenating Strings

In Swift, you can concatenate strings using the + operator:

```
var hello = "Hello"
var comma = ","
var world = "World"
var exclamation = "!"
var space = " "
var combinedStr = hello + comma + space + world + exclamation
println(combinedStr)  //---Hello, World!---
```

You can also use the *addition assignment operator* (+=) to append a string to another string:

```
var hello = "Hello"
hello += ", World!"
println(hello)   //---Hello, World!"
```

> **NOTE** *If you have an Objective-C background, the capability to append strings using the + operator is a very welcome feature.*

In the preceding examples, you are concatenating variables of the same type, which in this case is String. If you want to concatenate a String variable with variables of other types, there are a few things you need to note. Consider the following statements:

```
var euro:Character = "€"
var amount = 500
```

Here, euro is of type Character, and amount is of type Int. The easiest way to combine the two variables into a string is to use *string interpolation*. String interpolation has the following syntax:

```
\(variable_name)
```

The following statement uses string interpolation to combine the value of euro and amount into a single string:

```
var amountStr1 = "\(euro)\(amount)"
println(amountStr1)  //---€500---
```

If you try to concatenate a string together with a numeric value (such as Double or Int), you will get an error:

```
var amountStr2 = "\(euro)" + amount  //---error---
```

Instead, you should explicitly convert the numeric value to a string using the String() initializer:

```
var amountStr2 = "\(euro)" + String(amount)
```

Likewise, if you try to concatenate a `Character` type and an `Int` type, you will get a compiler error:

```
var amountStr3 = euro + amount   //---error---
```

As usual, you should convert both types to `String` before concatenating them:

```
var amountStr3 = String(euro) + String(amount)
```

Special Characters

String literals can contain one or more characters that have a special meaning in Swift.

If you want to represent the double quote (") within a string, prefix the double quote with a backslash (\\):

```
var quotation =
    "Albert Einstein: \"A person who never made a mistake never tried
    anything new\""
println(quotation)
```

The preceding statement outputs the following:

```
Albert Einstein: "A person who never made a mistake never tried anything
new"
```

If you want to represent the single quote (') within a string, simply include it in the string:

```
var str = "'A' for Apple"
println(str)
```

The preceding statement outputs the following:

```
'A' for Apple
```

If you want to represent the backslash (\\) within a string, prefix the backslash with another backslash (\\):

```
var path = "C:\\WINDOWS\\system32"
println(path)
```

The preceding statement outputs the following:

```
C:\WINDOWS\system32
```

The \t special character represents a tab character:

```
var headers = "Column 1 \t Column 2 \t Column3"
println(headers)
```

The preceding statement outputs the following:

```
Column 1     Column 2     Column3
```

The \n special character represents a newline character:

```
var column1 = "Row 1\nRow 2\nRow 3"
println(column1)
```

The preceding statement outputs the following:

```
Row 1
Row 2
Row 3
```

Unicode

In Swift, a `Character` represents a single *extended grapheme cluster*. An extended grapheme cluster is a sequence of one or more Unicode scalars that when combined produces a single human-readable character. Consider the following example:

```
let hand:Character = "\u{270B}"
let star = "\u{2b50}"
let bouquet = "\u{1F490}"
```

In the preceding code snippet, the three variables are of type `Character`, with the first one explicitly declared. Their values are assigned using *single Unicode scalars*, and when output they appear as shown in Figure 3-3.

> **NOTE** *Each Unicode scalar is a unique 21-bit number.*

FIGURE 3-3

Here is another example:

```
let aGrave = "\u{E0}"    //---à---
```

In the preceding statement, aGrave represents the Latin small letter "a" with a grave: à. The same statement can also be rewritten using a pair of scalars—the letter a followed by the COMBINING GRAVE ACCENT scalar:

```
let aGrave = "\u{61}\u{300}"
```

In either case, the aGrave variable contains *one* single character. To make this point clearer, consider the following statement:

```
var voila = "voila"
```

In the preceding statement, voila contains five characters. If you append the COMBINING GRAVE ACCENT scalar to it as follows, the voila variable would still contain five characters:

```
voila = "voila" + "\u{300}"  //--- voilà---
```

This is because the a has been changed to à.

COMMON STRING FUNCTIONS

When dealing with strings, you often need to perform the following operations:

➤   Test for string equality.

➤   Test if a string starts or ends with a particular string.

➤   Test if a string contains a particular string.

➤   Check the length of a string.

The following sections touch on these common string operations.

Equality

In Swift, string and character comparisons are performed using the *equal to* operator (==) or the *not equal to* operator (!=). Two strings are deemed to be equal if they contain *exactly the same Unicode scalars in the same order.* Here is an obvious example:

```
var string1 = "I am a string!"
var string2 = "I am a string!"
println(string1 == string2)  //---true---
println(string1 != string2)  //---false---
```

The following example shows a comparison between two `Character` variables, each containing a Unicode character:

```
var s1 = "é"        //---é---
var s2 = "\u{E9}"   //---é---
println(s1 == s2)  //---true---
```

The next example shows a comparison between two `String` variables, each including a Unicode character:

```
var s3 = "café"       //---café---
var s4 = "caf\u{E9}"  //---café---
println(s3 == s4)     //---true---
```

If you use a COMBINING ACUTE ACCENT scalar and apply it to the scalar that precedes it, the string would be different from one that does not use the COMBINING ACUTE ACCENT scalar, as the following code snippet shows:

```
var s5 = "voilà"             //--- voilà---
var s6 = "voila" + "\u{300}" //--- voila + `---
println(s5 == s6)            //---false---

let s7 = "\u{E0}"            //---à---
let s8 = "\u{61}\u{300}"     //---a + `---
println(s7 == s8)            //---false---
```

Prefix and Suffix

If you want to check if a string starts with a particular string prefix, use the `hasPrefix()` method:

```
var url: String = "www.apple.com"
var prefix = "http://"
if !url.hasPrefix(prefix) {
    url = prefix + url
}
println(url)
```

In the preceding code snippet, the `hasPrefix()` method takes in a `String` argument and returns `true` if the string contains the specified string prefix.

Likewise, you can use the `hasSuffix()` method to check whether a string contains a particular string suffix:

```
var url2 = "https://developer.apple.com/library/prerelease/ios/" +
           "documentation/General/Reference/" +
           "SwiftStandardLibraryReference/"

var suffix = "/"
if url2.hasSuffix(suffix) {
    println("URL ends with \(suffix)")
} else {
    println("URL does not end with \(suffix)")
}
```

The `hasPrefix()` and `hasSuffix()` methods work correctly with Unicode characters as well:

```
var str = "voila" + "\u{300}" //--- voila + `---
var suffix = "à"
if str.hasSuffix(suffix) {
    println("String ends with \(suffix)")
} else {
    println("String does not end with \(suffix)")
}
```

The preceding code snippet outputs the following:

```
String ends with à
```

Length

In Objective-C, you get the length/size of a string using the `length` property. However, in Swift, because Unicode characters do not take up the same unit of storage in memory, calling the `length` property on a string will not work (the `length` property is based on 16-bit code units). There are two ways to go about finding the length of a string in Swift:

➤   Use the equivalent of the `length` property (from `NSString`) in Swift. The `length` property from `NSString` is now wrapped in Swift and available as the `utf16Count` property. This approach is useful if you are not dealing with Unicode characters in your string.

➤ Use the `length` property in `NSString` directly. You can declare a string as an `NSString` instance and call the length property directly, or use the `bridgeToObjectiveC()` method to convert a `String` instance to an `NSString` instance.

➤ Use the global `countElements()` function available in Swift to count the length/size of a string. The `countElements()` function counts the size of Unicode characters correctly.

> **NOTE** The section "Interoperability with NSString" discusses using `NSString` in Swift in more detail.

Following are several examples. First, consider this statement:

```
let bouquet:Character = "\u{1F490}"
```

Because `bouquet` is declared as a `Character`, you will not be able to use the `countElements()` function (the `countElements()` function only works for strings):

```
println(countElements(bouquet))   //---error---
```

The following statements each output 1 for the length of the strings:

```
var s1 = "é"              //---é---
println(countElements(s1))   //---1---

var s2 = "\u{E9}"          //---é---
println(countElements(s2))   //---1---
```

Whether you use a Unicode character directly or use a Unicode scalar within your string, the length of the string is still the same:

```
var s3 = "café"            //---café---
println(countElements(s3))   //---4---

var s4 = "caf\u{E9}"       //---café---
println(countElements(s4))   //---4---
```

Even if you combine a Unicode scalar with a string, the `countElements()` function will still count the number of characters correctly, as the following statements show:

```
var s5 = "voilà"           //--- voilà---
println(countElements(s5))   //---5---

var s6 = "voila" + "\u{300}" //--- voila + `---
println(countElements(s6))   //---5---
```

Substrings

One of the most common operations you perform with a string is that of extracting part of it, commonly known as a substring. Unfortunately, due to the support of Unicode characters in the

String type, extracting strings from a String type is not so straightforward. This section provides an explanation of how to go about extracting part of a string.

First, consider the following swiftString:

```
let swiftString:String =
    "The quick brown fox jumps over the lazy dog."
```

Every String type has a number of properties of type String.Index. Index is a structure that contains a number of properties that point to the current character in the String variable, its next character, its previous character, and so on. The Index structure is defined as an extension to the String type:

```
extension String : Collection {
    struct Index : BidirectionalIndex, Reflectable {
        func successor() -> String.Index
        func predecessor() -> String.Index
        func getMirror() -> Mirror
    }
    var startIndex: String.Index { get }
    var endIndex: String.Index { get }
    subscript (i: String.Index) -> Character { get }
    func generate() -> IndexingGenerator<String>
}
```

To better understand the use of the Index structure, consider the following statement:

```
println(swiftString[swiftString.startIndex])   //---T---
```

The preceding statement uses the startIndex property (of type String.Index) to refer to the first character of the string. You use it as the index to pass to the String's subscript() method to extract the first character. Note that due to the way characters are stored in the String variable, you cannot directly specify a number indicating the position of the character that you want to extract, like this:

```
println(swiftString[0])   //---error---
```

You can also use the endIndex property together with the predecessor() method to get the last character in the string:

```
println(swiftString[swiftString.endIndex.predecessor()])     //---.---
```

To get the character at a particular index, you can use the advance() method and specify the number of characters to move relative to a starting position:

```
//---start from the string's startIndex and advance 2 characters---
var index = advance(swiftString.startIndex, 2)
println(swiftString[index])   //---e---
```

In the preceding statements, index is of type String.Index. You make use of it to extract the character from the string.

You can also traverse the string backwards by starting at the end index and specifying a negative value to move:

```
index = advance(swiftString.endIndex, -3)
println(swiftString[index])   //---o---
```

The `successor()` method returns the position of the character after the current character:

```
println(swiftString[index.successor()])    //---g---
```

The `predecessor()` method returns the position of the character prior to the current character:

```
println(swiftString[index.predecessor()])   //---d---
```

You can also use the `subStringFromIndex()` method to obtain a substring starting from the specified index:

```
println(swiftString.substringFromIndex(index))
//---e quick brown fox jumps over the lazy dog.---
```

Likewise, to get the substring from the beginning up to the specified index, use the `substringToIndex()` method:

```
println(swiftString.substringToIndex(index))   //---Th---
```

What if you want to find a range within the string? You can use the following code snippet:

```
//---creates a Range<Int> instance; start index at 4 and end at 8---
let r = Range(start: 4, end: 8)

//---create a String.Index instance to point to the starting char---
let startIndex = advance(swiftString.startIndex, r.startIndex)

//---create a String.Index instance to point to the end char---
let endIndex = advance(startIndex, r.endIndex - r.startIndex + 1)

//---create a Range<String.Index> instance---
var range = Range(start: startIndex, end: endIndex)

//---extract the substring using the Range<String.Index> instance---
println(swiftString.substringWithRange(range))   //---quick---
```

The preceding code snippet uses the `substringWithRange()` method to extract the characters starting from index 4 and ending at index 8. The `substringWithRange()` method takes in a `Range<String.Index>` instance, so you need to write a little code to create it.

If you want to find the position of a character within a string, you can use the `find()` method:

```
//---finding the position of a character in a string---
let char:Character = "i"
if let charIndex = find(swiftString, char) {
    let charPosition = distance(swiftString.startIndex, charIndex)
```

```
        println(charPosition)  //---6---
    }
```

The `find()` method returns a `String.Index` instance. In order to translate that into an integer, you need to use the `distance()` method.

Converting Strings to Arrays

Another way to deal with a string's individual character is to convert a `String` value into an array. The following statement shows `str` containing a string with a Unicode character:

```
var str = "voila" + "\u{300}" //--- voila + `---
```

You can convert the string into an `Array` instance:

```
var arr = Array(str)
```

Once the string is converted to an array, you can access its individual characters through its index:

```
println(arr[4])    //---à---
```

Type Conversion

In Swift, there is no implicit conversion; you need to perform explicit conversion whenever you want to convert a variable from one type to another type. Consider the following statement:

```
var s1 = "400"
```

By type inherence, `s1` is `String`. If you want to convert it into an `Int` type, you need to use the `toInt()` method to explicitly convert it:

```
var amount1:Int? = s1.toInt()
```

You must specify the `?` character to indicate that this is an optional type; otherwise, the type conversion will fail. You can rewrite the preceding example to use type inference:

```
var amount1 = s1.toInt()
```

Consider another example:

```
var s2 = "1.25"
```

If you call the `toInt()` method to explicitly convert it to the `Int` type, you will get a `nil`:

```
var amount2 = s2.toInt()    //---nil as string cannot be converted to Int---
```

If you call the `toDouble()` method to explicitly convert it to the `Double` type, you will get an error:

```
var amount2:Double = s2.toDouble()  //---error---
```

This is because the `String` type does not have the `toDouble()` method. To resolve this, you can cast it to `NSString` and use the `doubleValue` property:

```
var amount2: Double = (s2 as NSString).doubleValue  //---1.25---
```

> **NOTE** The next section, "Interoperability with NSString," discusses this in more detail.

What about converting from numeric values to `String` types? Consider the following code snippet:

```
var num1 = 200    //---num1 is Int---
var num2 = 1.25   //---num2 is Double---
```

To convert the `num1` (which is of type `Int`), you can use the `String` initializer:

```
var s3 = String(num1)
```

Alternatively, you can use the string interpolation method:

```
var s3 = "\(num1)"
```

To convert the `num2` (which is of type `Double`), you cannot use the `String` initializer, as it does not accept an argument of type `Double`:

```
var s4 = String(num2)    //---error---
```

Instead, you have to use the string interpolation method:

```
var s4 = "\(num2)"
```

INTEROPERABILITY WITH NSSTRING

If you are familiar with the `NSString` class in Objective-C, you will be happy to know that the `String` type in Swift is bridged seamlessly (almost) with the `NSString` class in the Foundation framework in Objective-C. This means that you can continue to use the methods and properties related to `NSString` in Swift's `String` type. However, there are some caveats that you need to be aware of.

Consider the following statement:

```
var str1 = "This is a Swift string"
```

Based on type inference, `str1` would be of `String` type. However, you can continue to use the methods and properties already available in `NSString`, such as the following properties:

```
println(str1.uppercaseString)
println(str1.lowercaseString)
println(str1.capitalizedString)
```

In the preceding statements, `uppercaseString`, `lowercaseString`, and `capitalizedString` are all properties belonging to the `NSString` class, but you can use them in a `String` instance.

Swift will also automatically convert a result from `NSArray` of `NSString`s to the `Array` class in Swift, as the following example demonstrates:

```
var fruitsStr = "apple,orange,pineapple,durian"
var fruits = fruitsStr.componentsSeparatedByString(",")
for fruit in fruits {
    println(fruit)
}
```

The preceding code snippet extracts from the string an array of items separated by the comma (,). The result of type `NSArray` is automatically converted to the `Array` type in Swift. The preceding example will output the following:

```
apple
orange
pineapple
durian
```

Casting String to NSString

There are some methods from the `NSString` class that you need to take note of in Swift. For example, the `containsString()` method is available in `NSString`, but if you call it directly in an instance of the `String` type, you will get an error:

```
var str1 = "This is a Swift string"
println(str1.containsString("Swift"))
//---error: 'String' does not have a member named 'containsString'---
```

For such cases, you first need to explicitly convert the `String` instance to an `NSString` instance using the as keyword:

```
var str1 = "This is a Swift string"
println((str1 as NSString).containsString("Swift"))  //---true---
```

Once you have converted the `String` instance to an `NSString` instance, you can call the `containsString()` method.

As described earlier in the chapter, due to the way characters are stored in a `String` instance, you have to use the `countElements()` method in Swift to get the length of a string. However, you can also use the `length` property available in the `NSString` class by type casting it to `NSString`:

```
var str1 = "This is a Swift string"
println((str1 as NSString).length)  //---22---
```

Another thing to be aware of is that some methods require arguments to be of a particular Swift type, even if the method is available in `NSString`. For example, the `stringByReplacingCharactersInRange()` method takes in two arguments: an instance of type

Range<String.Index> and a string instance. If you call this method and pass in an NSRange instance, an error will occur:

```
//---an instance of NSRange---
var nsRange = NSMakeRange(5, 2)

str1.stringByReplacingCharactersInRange(nsRange, withString: "was")
//---error: 'NSRange' is not convertible to 'Range<String.Index>'---
```

Instead, you need to create an instance of type Range<String.Index> (a Swift type) and use it in the stringByReplacingCharactersInRange() method:

```
//---an instance of Range<String.Index>---
var swiftRange =
    advance(str1.startIndex, 5) ..< advance(str1.startIndex, 7)

str1 = str1.stringByReplacingCharactersInRange(
    swiftRange, withString: "was")
println(str1)    //---This was a Swift string---
```

> **NOTE** *The ..< operator is known as the* half-open range operator. *It has this syntax:* a ..< b, *which specifies a range of values from* a *to* b, *but not including* b. *The* half-open range operator *is discussed in more details in Chapter 4.*

Using NSString Directly

An alternative way to deal with strings is to declare a variable explicitly as an NSString type:

```
var str2:NSString = "This is a NSString in Objective-C. "
```

In the preceding statement, str2 will now be an NSString instance. The statement can also be rewritten as follows:

```
var str2 = "This is a NSString in Objective-C. " as NSString
```

You can call all the NSString methods directly via str2:

```
println(str2.length)                    //---35---
println(str2.containsString("NSString")) //---true---
println(str2.hasPrefix("This"))          //---true---
println(str2.hasSuffix(". "))            //---true---
println(str2.uppercaseString)   //---THIS IS A NSSTRING IN OBJECTIVE-C.---
println(str2.lowercaseString)   //---this is a nsstring in objective-c.---
println(str2.capitalizedString) //---This Is A Nsstring In Objective-C---

println(str2.stringByAppendingString("Yeah!"))
//---This is a NSString in Objective-C. Yeah!---

println(str2.stringByAppendingFormat("This is a number: %d", 123))
//---This is a NSString in Objective-C. This is a number: 123---
```

You can also create an `NSRange` instance and use it directly in the `stringByReplacingCharactersInRange()` method:

```
var range = str2.rangeOfString("Objective-C")
if range.location != NSNotFound {
    println("Index is \(range.location) length is \(range.length)")
    //---Index is 22 length is 11---
    str2 = str2.stringByReplacingCharactersInRange(
    range, withString: "Swift")
    println(str2)  //---This is a NSString in Swift.---
}
```

Here is another example of using the `rangeOfString()` method from `NSString` to find the index of the occurrence of a string within a string:

```
var path:NSString = "/Users/wei-menglee/Desktop"

//---find the index of the last /---
range = path.rangeOfString("/",
    options:NSStringCompareOptions.BackwardsSearch)

if range.location != NSNotFound {
    println("Index is \(range.location)")  //---18---
}
```

String or NSString?

Now that you are aware of the two possible ways to deal with strings in Swift, which one should you use?

As a rule of thumb, use the `String` type in Swift whenever possible and feasible. The Swift language is optimized to use the `String` type and in most cases, you can pass a `String` type into methods that expect an `NSString` type.

If you are dealing with special characters such as *emoji* or Chinese characters that take up two or three bytes, it is always better to use the native `String` type in Swift. For example, consider the following statement:

```
let bouquet = "\u{1F490}"
```

In the preceding statement, `bouquet` contains a single emoji (a bouquet graphic). It occupies two bytes of storage. If you want to count the number of characters contained within the string, the `countElements()` method counts it correctly:

```
println(countElements("\(bouquet)"))    //---1---
```

However, if you use the `NSString`'s `length` property, it returns the storage required instead of the number of characters contained within the string:

```
println((bouquet as NSString).length)  //---2---
```

Likewise, in one of the examples earlier in the chapter, if you append the COMBINING GRAVE ACCENT scalar to a string, the countElements() method will count the characters correctly, whereas the length property does not:

```
var s6 = "voila" + "\u{300}"       //--- voila + `---
println(countElements(s6))         //---5---
println((s6 as NSString).length)   //---6---
```

Using the native String type also enables you to use the various string features (such as string concatenation using the + operator, the For-In loop for character iteration, etc.) introduced in Swift. Once you explicitly declare a variable as NSString, you lose all these features. For example, for NSString types you cannot concatenate strings using the + operator:

```
var s:NSString =  "Swift"
s += " Programming"    //---not allowed---
```

Nor can you cannot iterate through an NSString using the For-In loop:

```
var s:NSString =  "Swift"
for c in s {
    println(c)
}
```

If you want to have the best of both worlds, always create a native String instance and then typecast to NSString to call the NSString's methods whenever necessary.

> **NOTE** There is another good reason to use the native String type. If Swift is ever ported to a non-Apple platform, the Foundation framework may not be available for your use. Therefore, your code that relies on the NSString methods will now likely break.

SUMMARY

In this chapter, you have learned about the String type in Swift and how it interoperates with the NSString class, with which most Objective-C developers are familiar. While you may be tempted to use the various string libraries that you are already familiar with in Objective-C, it is always a good idea to familiarize yourself with the various String methods in Swift so that your code is future-proof. Also, as the Swift language evolves, you should be seeing more enhancements to the language as Apple ramps up adoption of the language.

EXERCISES

1. Given the following statement, write the solution to find out the position of the "q" character in the string:

```
var str1 = "The quick brown fox jumps over the lazy dog"
```

2. The following code snippet causes the compiler to flag an error. Fix it.

```
var amount = "1200"
var rate = "1.27"
var result = amount * rate
```

3. Given the following variables, write the statement to output the following:

```
var lat = 40.765819
var lng = -73.975866
println("<fill in the blanks>")
// Lat/Lng is (40.765819, -73.975866)
```

► WHAT YOU LEARNED IN THIS CHAPTER

TOPIC	KEY CONCEPTS
Representing a string	You can represent a string using the `String` or `NSString` type.
Mutability of strings	Strings created using the `let` keyword are immutable. Strings created using the `var` keyword are mutable.
String as a value type	Strings are represented as a value type in Swift; when they are assigned to another variable/constant, a copy is made.
Representing characters	You can represent a character using the `Character` type.
Concatenating strings	Strings can be conveniently concatenated using the + or += operator.
Unicode	The `String` type in Swift is capable of representing Unicode characters.
String equality	To test the equality of two strings, use the == or != operator.
Length of a string	To find out the length of a string, you can either cast it to a `NSString` and then use the `length` property, or you can use the `countElements()` function in Swift.
Converting a string to an array	Another way to deal with a string is to convert it into an array.
String to number conversion	Use the `toInt()` method to convert a string to an integer. To convert a string into a double, cast the string to `NSString` and then use the `doubleValue` property.
Casting from `String` to `NSString`	Use the `as` keyword to cast a `String` to `NSString`.

Basic Operators

WHAT YOU WILL LEARN IN THIS CHAPTER:

➤ How to assign values to variables and constants using the assignment operator

➤ How to perform arithmetic operations using the arithmetic operators

➤ How to increment and decrement variables by one using the increment and decrement operators

➤ Using increment and decrement variables using the compound assignment operators

➤ How to use the nil coalescing operator when dealing with optional types

➤ How to perform comparisons using the comparison operators

➤ How to specify ranges using the range operator

➤ How to perform logical comparisons using the logical operators

In the previous two chapters you learned about the various data types in Swift and how Swift deals with strings and characters. In this chapter, you will learn about the various operators available in Swift. Operators work with the various data types to enable you to make logical decisions, perform arithmetical calculations, as well as change values. Swift supports the following types of operators:

➤ Assignment

➤ Arithmetic

➤ Comparison

➤ Range

➤ Logical

ASSIGNMENT OPERATOR

The assignment operator (=) sets a variable or constant to a value. In Swift, you can create a constant by assigning a value to a constant name as shown here:

```
let companyName = "Developer Learning Solutions"
let factor = 5
```

You can also create a variable using the assignment operator:

```
var customerName1 = "Richard"
```

Besides assigning a value to a variable or constant, you can also assign a variable or constant to another:

```
var customerName2 = customerName1
```

You can also assign a tuple directly to a variable or constant:

```
let pt1 = (3,4)
```

> **NOTE** *Tuples are discussed in more detail in Chapter 2.*

You can decompose the value of a tuple into multiple variables or constants by using the assignment operator:

```
let (x,y) = (5,6)
println(x)    //---5---
println(y)    //---6---
```

Unlike Objective-C, the assignment operator does not return a value; hence, you cannot do something like this:

```
//---error---
if num = 5 {
    ...
}
```

This is a good feature, as it prevents programmers from accidentally doing an assignment instead of an equality comparison.

ARITHMETIC OPERATORS

Swift supports the four standard arithmetic operators:

➤ Addition (+)

➤ Subtraction (-)

➤ Multiplication (*)

➤ Division (/)

Swift requires the operands in all arithmetic operations to be of the same type. This enforces type safety, as it requires you to explicitly perform type casting. Consider the following statements:

```
var a = 9      //---Int---
var b = 4.1    //---Double---
```

By using type inference, a is `Int` and b is `Double`. Because they are of different types, the following operations are not allowed:

```
println(a * b)  //---error---
println(a / b)  //---error---
println(a + b)  //---error---
println(a - b)  //---error---
```

You need to convert the variables to be of the same type before you can perform arithmetic operations on them.

Addition Operator

The addition operator (+) adds two numbers together. When adding numeric values, you need to be aware of some important subtleties. First, integer addition is straightforward:

```
println(5 + 6)        //---integer addition (11)---
```

If you add a double to an integer, the result is a double:

```
println(5.1 + 6)      //---double addition (11.1)---
```

If you add two doubles, the result is a double:

```
println(5.1 + 6.2)    //---double addition (11.3)---
```

Besides adding numbers, the addition operator can also be used to concatenate two strings:

```
//---string concatenation (Hello, World)---
println("Hello, " + "World")
```

The addition operator can also be used as a *unary plus operator* (it operates on only one operand):

```
var num1 = 8
var anotherNum1 = +num1   //---anotherNum1 is 8---
```

```
var num2 = -9
var anotherNum2 = +num2    //---anotherNum2 is -9
```

For the additional operator, using it as a unary plus operator is redundant—it does not change the value or the sign of the number. However, it is useful as an aid to improve code readability.

Subtraction Operator

The subtraction operator (-) enables you to subtract one number from another. As with the addition operator, you need to be aware of its behavior when subtracting two numbers of different types.

The following subtracts an integer from another:

```
println(7 - 8)        //---integer subtraction (-1)---
```

If you subtract an integer from a double, the result is a double:

```
println(9.1 - 5)      //---double subtraction (4.1)---
```

However, when you subtract a double from an integer, the result is a double:

```
println(9 - 4.1)      //---double subtraction (4.9)---
```

Like the addition operator, the subtraction operator can also be used as a unary operator to indicate a negative number:

```
println(-25)          //---negative number---
```

It can also be used to negate the value of a variable:

```
var positiveNum = 5
var negativeNum = -positiveNum   //---negativeNum is now -5---
positiveNum = -negativeNum        //---positiveNum is now 5---
```

Multiplication Operator

The multiplication operator (*) multiplies two numbers. Like the addition and subtraction operators, multiplying numbers of different types yields results of different types, as the following demonstrates.

Multiplying two integer numbers results in an integer result:

```
println(3 * 4)        //---integer multiplication (12)---
```

Multiplying a double value with an integer value also results in a double result:

```
println(3.1 * 4)      //---double multiplication (12.4)---
```

When you multiply two double values you get a double result:

```
println(3.1 * 4.0)    //---double multiplication (12.4)---
```

Division Operator

The division operator (/) divides a number by another number. Dividing an integer by another integer will return only the integer part of the result:

```
println(5 / 6)       //---integer division (0)---
println(6 / 5)       //---integer division (1)---
```

Dividing a double by an integer will return a double:

```
println(6.1 / 5)     //---double division (1.22)---
println(9.99 / 5)    //---double division (1.998)---
```

Dividing a double by a double will return a double:

```
println(6.1 / 5.5)   //---double division (1.10909090909091)---
```

Modulus Operator

The modulus operator (%) returns the remainder of a division. For example, if you divide five by three, the remainder is two. The following shows how the % operator works:

```
println(8 % 9)       //---modulo (8)---
println(9 % 8)       //---modulo (1)---
println(9 % 9)       //---modulo (0)---
```

The modulus operator also works with a negative number:

```
println(-5 % 3)      //---module (-2)---
```

If the second operand is a negative number, the negative value is always ignored:

```
//---negative value for second number is always ignored---
println(-5 % -3)     //---module (-2)---
```

The modulus operator also works with double values:

```
println(5 % 3.5)     //---module (1.5)---
println(5.9 % 3.5)   //---module (2.4)---
```

Increment and Decrement Operators

Because it is a very common task in programming to increment or decrement the value of a variable by one, Swift provides the increment (++) and decrement (--) operators as a shortcut to these operations. For example, if you want to increment the value of a variable by one, you typically do this:

```
var i = 5
i = i + 1  //---i is now 6---
```

However, using the increment operator, you can rewrite the preceding code as follows:

```
var i = 5
++i          //---i is now 6---
```

Both the increment and decrement operators can be used as either a *prefix* or a *postfix* operator. Let's take a look at the increment operator first:

```
i = 5
++i    //---i is now 6---
i++    //---i is now 7---
```

In the preceding example, i has an initial value of 5. Using the ++ as a prefix operator (i.e., ++i) as well as a postfix operator (i.e., i++) yields no difference—the value of i will be increased by one. However, if you use the increment or decrement operator in an assignment statement, you need to be aware of the subtle difference between using it as a prefix or postfix operator. The following example makes this clear:

```
i = 5
var j = i++   //---j is now 5, i is now 6---
println(i)    //---6---
println(j)    //---5---
```

In the preceding example, when you use the ++ as a postfix operator, its *initial* value (which is currently 5) is retrieved and assigned to j, after which the value of i is incremented by one (which is 6 after the incrementing).

What about using the ++ as a prefix operator? Consider the following example:

```
i = 5
j = ++i       //---both i and j are now 6---
println(i)    //---6---
println(j)    //---6---
```

Here, using the ++ as a prefix operator will immediately increment the value of i by one (6 after incrementing). The value of i is then assigned to j (which is now 6).

The same behavior of the postfix and prefix operators applies to the -- operator as well, as the following code snippet shows:

```
i = 5
j = i--       //---j is now 5, i is now 4---
println(i)    //---4---
println(j)    //---5---


i = 5
j = --i       //---both i and j are now 4---
println(i)    //---4---
println(j)    //---4---
```

Compound Assignment Operators

Compound assignment operators combine the assignment (=) operator with another operator:

```
var salary = 2000
salary = salary + 1200   //---salary is now 3200---
```

In the preceding example, the value of salary is incremented by 1200. This statement could be rewritten using the compound assignment operator +=:

```
salary += 1200   //---salary is now 3200---
```

The following shows some additional compound assignment operators in use:

```
var speed = 80
speed -= 15      //---speed is now 65---

var size = 2
size *= 3        //---size is now 6---

var width = 100
width /= 2       //---width is now 50---
```

Nil Coalescing Operator

Consider the following optional variable:

```
var gender:String?
```

The gender variable is an optional variable that can take a String value or a nil value. Suppose you want to assign the value of gender to another variable, and if it contains nil, you will assign a default value to the variable. Your code may look like this:

```
var genderOfCustomer:String

if gender == nil {
    genderOfCustomer = "male"
} else {
    genderOfCustomer = gender!
}
```

Here you check whether gender is nil. If it is, you assign a default value of "male" to genderOfCustomer. If gender is not nil, then its value is assigned to genderOfCustomer.

Swift introduces the new *nil coalescing operator*, which has the following syntax: a ?? b. It reads "unwrap the value of optional *a* and return its value if it is not nil; otherwise, return *b*."

The preceding code snippet could be rewritten in a single statement using the new nil coalescing operator:

```
var gender:String?
var genderOfCustomer = gender ?? "male"    //---male---
```

Because gender is nil, genderOfCustomer is now assigned male.

If you now assign a value to gender and execute the preceding statements again, gender would be female:

```
var gender:String? = "female"
var genderOfCustomer = gender ?? "male"   //---female---
```

COMPARISON OPERATORS

Swift supports the standard comparison operators available in most programming languages:

➤   Equal to (==)

➤   Not equal to (!=)

➤   Less than (<)

➤   Less than or equal to (<=)

➤   Greater than (>)

➤   Greater than or equal to (>=)

Equal To and Not Equal To

To check for the equality of two variables, you can use the *equal to* (==) operator. The == operator works with numbers as well as strings. Consider the following example:

```
var n = 6
if n % 2 == 1 {
    println("Odd number")
} else {
    println("Even number")
}
```

The preceding code snippet checks whether the remainder of a number divided by two is equal to one. If it is, then the number is an odd number, otherwise it is an even number.

The following example shows the == operator comparing string values:

```
var status = "ready"
if status == "ready" {
    println("Machine is ready")
} else {
    println("Machine is not ready")
}
```

Besides the == operator, you can also use the *not equal to* (!=) operator. The following code snippet shows the earlier example rewritten using the != operator:

```
var n = 6
if n % 2 != 1 {
    println("Even number")
} else {
```

```
        println("Odd number")
    }
```

Likewise, you can also use the `!=` operator for string comparisons:

```
var status = "ready"
if status != "ready" {
    println("Machine is not ready")
} else {
    println("Machine is ready")
}
```

The `==` and `!=` operators also work with Character types:

```
let char1:Character = "A"
let char2:Character = "B"
let char3:Character = "B"
println(char1 == char2) //---false---
println(char2 == char3) //---true---
println(char1 != char2) //---true---
println(char2 != char3) //---false---
```

> **NOTE** *When comparing instances of classes, you need to use the* identity *operators (=== and !==). Identity operators are discussed in Chapter 8.*

Greater Than or Equal To

To determine whether a number is greater than another number, use the *greater than* (>) operator:

```
println(5 > 5)  //---false---
println(5 > 6)  //---false---
println(6 > 5)  //---true---
```

You can also use the *greater than or equal to* (>=) operator:

```
println(7 >= 7) //---true---
println(7 >= 8) //---false---
println(9 >= 8) //---true---
```

> **NOTE** *The* > *and* >= *operators do not work with the* String *type.*

Less Than or Equal To

To determine whether a number is less than another number, use the *less than* (<) operator:

```
println(4 < 4)  //---false---
println(4 < 5)  //---true---
println(5 < 4)  //---false---
```

You can also use the *less than or equal to* (>=) operator:

```
println(8 <= 8) //---true---
println(9 <= 8) //---false---
println(7 <= 8) //---true---
```

The < operator also work with strings:

```
println("abc" < "ABC") //---false---
println("123a" < "123b") //---true---
```

> **NOTE** *The* <= *operator does not work with the* String *type.*

RANGE OPERATORS

Swift supports two types of range operators to specify a range of values:

➤ **Closed range operator (a. . .b)**—Specifies a range of values starting from *a* right up to *b* (inclusive)

➤ **Half-open range operator (a. .<b)**—Specifies a range of values starting from *a* right up to *b*, but not including *b*

To demonstrate how these range operators work, consider the following example:

```
//---prints 5 to 9 inclusive---
for num in 5...9 {
    println(num)
}
```

The preceding code snippet uses the closed range operator to output all the numbers from 5 to 9:

```
5
6
7
8
9
```

To output only 5 to 8, you can use the half-open range operator:

```
//---prints 5 to 8---
for num in 5..<9 {
    println(num)
}
```

The preceding code snippet outputs 5 to 8:

```
5
6
```

```
7
8
```

The half-open range operator is particularly useful when you are dealing with zero-based lists such as arrays. The following code snippet is one good example:

```
//---useful for 0-based lists such as arrays---
var fruits = ["apple","orange","pineapple","durian","rambutan"]
for n in 0..<fruits.count {
    println(fruits[n])
}
```

The preceding code snippet outputs the following:

```
apple
orange
pineapple
durian
rambutan
```

LOGICAL OPERATORS

Like most programming languages, Swift supports three logical operators:

➤ Logical NOT (!)

➤ Logical AND (&&)

➤ Logical OR (||)

NOT

The logical NOT (!) operator inverts a `Bool` value so that `true` becomes `false` and `false` becomes `true`.

The following table shows how the NOT operator works on a value:

a	!a
true	false
false	true

Consider the following statement:

```
var happy = true
```

The variable `happy` is of type `Bool` and is set to `true`. To invert the value of `happy`, use the logical NOT operator:

```
happy = !happy
```

The value of `happy` is now `false`. You can use the logical NOT operator in an If condition, like the following:

```
if !happy {
    println("Cheer up man!")
}
```

The preceding reads: "If NOT happy, then print the line …" Because the value of happy is `false`, the NOT operator negates it and returns a `true` value, which satisfies the If condition. Therefore, the line is printed.

As you can see in this example, using the appropriate name for your variables can greatly aid in the readability of your code.

AND

The logical AND operator creates a logical expression (a `&&` b) where both a and b must be `true` in order to evaluate to `true`.

The following table shows how the AND operator works on two values. As you can see, both a and b must be `true` in order for the expression to be `true`.

a	b	a && b
true	true	true
true	false	false
false	true	false
false	false	false

Consider the following example:

```
var happy = true
var raining = false

if happy && !raining {
    println("Let's go for a picnic!")
}
```

In the preceding example, the line "Let's go for a picnic!" will only be printed if you are happy and it is not raining.

Note that Swift does not require you to wrap an expression using a pair of parentheses (needed in Objective-C), but you can always add it for readability:

```
if (happy && !raining) {
    println("Let's go for a picnic!")
}
```

Swift supports *short-circuit evaluation* for evaluating the AND expression—if the first value is `false`, the second value will not be evaluated because the logical AND operator requires both values to be `true`.

OR

The logical OR operator creates a logical expression (a || b) where either a or b needs to be true in order to evaluate to true.

The following table shows how the OR operator works on two values. As you can see, as long as either a or b is true, the expression evaluates to true.

a	b	a || b
true	true	true
true	false	true
false	true	true
false	false	false

Consider the following example:

```
var age = 131
if age > 130 || age < 1 {
    println("Age is out of range")
}
```

In the preceding example, the line "Age is out of range" will be printed if age is more than 130 or less than 1. In this case, the line is printed, as age is 131.

Combining Logical Operators

While the logical operators work with two operands, it is common to combine them together in a single expression, as shown in the following example:

```
var condition1 = false
var condition2 = true
var condition3 = true

if condition1 && condition2 || condition3 {
    println("Do something")
}
```

In this example, the first condition is evaluated first:

condition1 (false) **&& condition2** (true)

It then takes the result of the evaluation (which is false) and evaluates it with the next operand:

false || **condition3** (true)

The result of this expression is true, and the line "Do something" is printed.

Sometimes, however, you may not want the evaluation of the expressions to go from left to right. Consider the following example:

```
var happy = false
```

```
var skyIsClear = true
var weatherIsGood = true
```

Suppose you want to go out only if you are happy and the sky is either clear or the weather is good. In this case you would write the expression as follows:

```
if happy && (skyIsClear || weatherIsGood) {
    println("Let's go out!")
}
```

Note the parentheses in the expression:

```
(skyIsClear || weatherIsGood)
```

This expression needs to be evaluated first. In this example, it evaluates to `true`. Next, it evaluates with the first operand:

happy (false) **&&** true

The final expression evaluates to `false`, which means you are not going out today.

The next example doesn't use the parentheses:

```
happy && skyIsClear || weatherIsGood
```

Therefore, the preceding expression yields a different result:

```
happy (false) && skyIsClear (true) = false
false || weatherIsGood (true) = true
```

As a rule of thumb, use parentheses to group related conditions together so that they are evaluated first. Even if it is redundant sometimes, parentheses aid in the readability of your code.

Ternary Conditional Operator

Very often, you will use the If-Else statement to write simple statements like the following:

```
var day = 5
var openingTime:Int

if day == 6 || day == 7 {
    openingTime = 12
} else {
    openingTime = 9
}
```

In the preceding code snippet, you want to know the opening time (`openingTime`) of a store based on the day of the week (`day`). If it is Saturday (6) or Sunday (7), then the opening time is 12:00 noon; otherwise on the weekday it is 9:00 A.M. Such a statement could be shortened using the *ternary conditional operator*, as shown here:

```
openingTime = (day == 6 || day == 7) ? 12: 9
```

The ternary conditional operator has the following syntax:

```
variable = condition ? value_if_true : value_if_false
```

It first evaluates the *condition*. If the *condition* evaluates to `true`, the *value_if_true* is assigned to *variable*. Otherwise, the *value_if_false* is assigned to *variable*.

SUMMARY

In this chapter, you have seen the many operators supported in Swift. While some are standards in other languages, such as the logical, comparison, and arithmetic operators, some are new in Swift—such as the nil coalescing operator and the range operators. When using constant values with the arithmetic operators, you have to pay attention to data types and be sure to check the data type of the result if you are using a mixture of different types in your arithmetic operations.

EXERCISES

1. Write the output for the following code snippet:

    ```
    var num = 5
    var sum = ++num + num++

    println(num)
    println(sum)
    ```

2. Given the following array of numbers, write the code snippet to sum up all the odd numbers using the half-open range operator:

    ```
    var nums = [3,4,2,1,5,7,9,8]
    ```

3. Rewrite the following code snippet using the nil coalescing operator:

    ```
    var userInput = "5"
    var num = userInput.toInt()
    var value:Int
    if num == nil {
        value = 0
    } else {
        value = num!
    }
    ```

▶ **WHAT YOU LEARNED IN THIS CHAPTER**

TOPIC	KEY CONCEPTS
Assignment operation	Use the = operator.
Arithmetic operations	Use the +, -, *, and / operators.
Modulus operation	Use the % operator.
Increment and decrement operations	Use the ++ and -- operators.
Compound assignment operators	Use the +=, -=, *=, and /= operators.
Nil coalescing operator	*var c = a ?? b.*
Comparison operations	Use the ==, !=, <, <=, >, or >= operators.
Range operations	Use the closed range operator (a...b) or the half-open range operator (a..<b).
Logical operations	Use the !, &&, or || operators.
Ternary conditional operator	*variable = condition ?* *value_if_true : value_if_false.*

5

Functions

WHAT YOU WILL LEARN IN THIS CHAPTER:

➤   How to define and call a function

➤   How to define input parameters

➤   How to return a value or multiple values from a function

➤   How to define external parameter names

➤   How to define default parameter values

➤   How to define variadic parameters

➤   How to define constant and variable parameters

➤   How to define in-out parameters

➤   How to define and call function type variables

➤   How to return a function type from a function

➤   How to define nested functions

A *function* is a group of statements that perform a specific set of tasks. For example, a particular function may calculate the bonus of an employee based on a few parameters, such as his or her performance rating, number of years in the company, and so on. A function may also return a value, such as the amount of bonus to which an employee is entitled. In Swift, a function has a name, and it may also accept parameters and optionally return a value (or a set of values). Functions in Swift work similarly to traditional C functions, and they also support features such as external parameter names, which enables them to mirror the verbosity of Objective-C methods.

DEFINING AND CALLING A FUNCTION

In Swift, a function is defined using the `func` keyword, like this:

```
func doSomething() {
    println("doSomething")
}
```

The preceding code snippet defines a function called `doSomething`. It does not take in any inputs (known as *parameters*) and does not return a value (technically it does return a `Void` value).

To call the function, simply call its name followed by a pair of empty parentheses:

```
doSomething()
```

Input Parameters

A function can also optionally define one or more named typed inputs. The following function takes in *one single typed input parameter*:

```
func doSomething(num: Int) {
    println(num)
}
```

The `num` parameter is used internally within the function, and its data type is `Int`. To call this function, call its name and pass in an integer value (known as an *argument*), like this:

```
doSomething(5)
//---or---
var num = 5
doSomething(num)
```

The following function takes in two input parameters, both of type `Int`:

```
func doSomething(num1: Int, num2: Int) {
    println(num1, num2)
}
```

To call this function, pass it two integer values as the argument:

```
doSomething(5, 6)
```

Returning a Value

Functions are not required to return a value. However, if you want the function to return a value, use the `->` operator after the function declaration. The following function returns an integer value:

```
func doSomething(num1: Int, num2: Int, num3: Int) -> Int {
    return num1 + num2 + num3
}
```

You use the `return` keyword to return a value from a function and then exit it. When the function returns a value, you can assign it to a variable or constant, like this:

```
//---value returned from the function is assigned to a variable---
var sum = doSomething(5,6,7)
```

Return values from a function can also be ignored:

```
//---return value from a function is ignored---
doSomething(5,6,7)
```

Returning Multiple Values

Functions are not limited to returning a single value. In some cases, it is important for functions to return multiple values. In Swift, you can use a tuple type in a function to return multiple values. The following example shows a function that takes in a string containing numbers, examines each character in the string, and counts the number of odd and even numbers contained in it:

```
func countNumbers(string: String) -> (odd:Int, even:Int) {
    var odd = 0, even = 0
    for char in string {
        let digit = String(char).toInt()
        if (digit != nil) {
            (digit!) % 2 == 0 ? even++ : odd++
        }
    }
    return (odd, even)
}
```

The `(odd:Int, even:Int)` return type specifies the members of the tuple that would be returned by the function—odd (of type `Int`) and even (of type `Int`).

To use this function, pass it a string and assign the result to a variable or constant, like this:

```
var result = countNumbers("123456789")
```

The return result is stored as a tuple containing two integer members, named odd and even:

```
println("Odd: \(result.odd)")         //---5---
println("Even: \(result.even)")       //---4---
```

> **NOTE** The use of the ! character is known as forced unwrapping of an optional's value. For more information of the concept of optionals in Swift, refer to Chapter 2, "Data Types."

Function Parameter Names

So far in the previous discussion of functions with parameters, each parameter has a name. Take the example of this function shown previously:

```
func doSomething(num1: Int, num2: Int) {
    println(num1, num2)
}
```

In this example, `num1` and `num2` are the two parameters names for the function and they can only be used internally within the function. These are called *local parameter names*.

When calling this function, these two parameters names are not used at all:

```
doSomething(5, 6)
```

In more complex functions with multiple parameters, the use of each parameter is sometimes not obvious. Therefore, it would be useful to be able to name the parameter(s) when passing arguments to a function. In Swift, you can assign an *external parameter name* to individual parameters in a function. Consider the following example:

```
func doSomething(num1: Int, secondNum num2: Int) {

}
```

In this example, the second parameter is prefixed with an external parameter name `secondNum`. To call the function, you now need to specify the external parameter name, like this:

```
doSomething(5, secondNum:6)
```

> **NOTE** *If you define a function within a class (discussed in more details in Chapter 8), the second parameter onwards automatically becomes an external parameter name. In other words, there is no need to explicitly specify the external parameter names for the parameters (second parameter onwards) in the function declaration.*

You can also specify an external parameter name for the first parameter, such as the following:

```
func doSomething(firstNum num1: Int, secondNum num2: Int) {

}
```

In this case, you need to specify external parameter names for both parameters:

```
doSomething(firstNum:5, secondNum:6)
```

Figure 5-1 shows the difference between external and local parameter names.

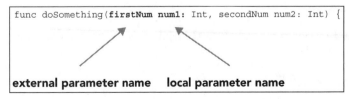

FIGURE 5-1

External parameter names are very useful for making function names descriptive. Consider the following examples of calling functions using external parameter names:

```
calculateDistance(point1, fromSecondPoint:point2)
printName(strName, withTitle:"Dr.")
joinString(str1, withString2:str2 andString3:str3 usingSeparator:",")
```

External Parameter Names Shorthand

Sometimes the local parameter name itself is descriptive enough to be used as an external parameter name. Consider the previous example:

```
func doSomething(num1: Int, num2: Int) {
    println(num1, num2)
}
```

Suppose you want to use num1 as the external parameter name for the first parameter and num2 for the second parameter. You could write it as follows:

```
func doSomething(num1 num1: Int, num2 num2: Int) {

}
```

Instead of repeating the parameter names twice, you could use the shorthand #, like this:

```
func doSomething(#num1: Int, #num2: Int) {

}
```

To call the function, you specify the external parameter names like this:

```
doSomething(num1:5, num2:6)
```

Default Parameter Values

You can assign a default value to a parameter so that it becomes optional when you are calling it. Consider the following function in which you have three parameters:

```
func joinName(firstName:String,
              lastName:String,
              joiner:String = " ") -> String {
    return "\(firstName)\(joiner)\(lastName)"
}
```

The third parameter has a default value of a single space. When calling this function with three arguments, you need to specify the default parameter name, like this:

```
var fullName = joinName("Wei-Meng", "Lee", joiner:",")
println(fullName)   //---Wei-Meng,Lee---
```

> **NOTE** For default parameters, you need to specify the parameter name explicitly when calling the function. In addition, for a default parameter, there is no need to specify an external parameter name or use the # shorthand when defining the function, as the default parameter implicitly indicates a named argument.

You can omit the default parameter when calling the function and it will use the default value of the single space for the third argument:

```
fullName = joinName("Wei-Meng","Lee")
println(fullName)    //---Wei-Meng Lee---
```

> **NOTE** Parameters with a default value must always be placed at the end of the parameter list.

You need to be careful when defining functions of the same name but with different input parameters. Consider the case where you have two functions both named `joinName` and the first one has a default parameter:

```
func joinName(firstName:String,
              lastName:String,
              joiner:String = " ") -> String {
    return "\(firstName)\(joiner)\(lastName)"
}

func joinName(firstName:String,
              lastName:String) -> String {
    return "\(firstName)\(lastName)"
}
```

To call the first function, you need to specify the external parameter name for the default parameter, like this:

```
var fullName = joinName("Wei-Meng", "Lee", joiner:",")
println(fullName)  //---Wei-Meng,Lee---
```

If you now call `joinName` by passing only two arguments, it will result in a compilation error because the compiler is not able to resolve which function to call:

```
var fullName = joinName("Wei-Meng","Lee")
```

Variadic (Variable) Parameters

In some situations you may need to define a function that accepts a variable number of arguments. For example, suppose you want to define a function that calculates the average of a series of numbers passed in as arguments. In this case your function can be defined as follows:

```
func average(nums: Int...) -> Float {
    var sum: Float = 0
    for num in nums {
        sum += Float(num)
    }
    return sum/Float(nums.count)
}
```

The . . . (three periods) indicates that the parameter accepts a varying number of arguments, which in this case are of type Int. A parameter that accepts a variable number of values is known as a *variadic* parameter. You can call the function by passing it arguments of any length:

```
println(average(1,2,3))      //---2.0---
println(average(1,2,3,4))    //---2.5---
println(average(1,2,3,4,5,6))  //---3.4---
```

> **NOTE** *A variadic parameter must appear last in the parameter list. Also, if you have a function that accepts default parameter values, the variadic parameter must be last in the parameter list.*

Constant and Variable Parameters

By default, all the parameters in a function are constants. In other words, your code within the function is not allowed to modify the parameter. The following illustrates this:

```
func doSomething(num: Int) {
    num++  //---this is illegal as num is a constant by default---
    println(num)
}
```

If you want to modify the value of a parameter, you can copy it out to another variable, like this:

```
func doSomething(num: Int) {
    var n = num
    n++
    println(n)
}
```

> **NOTE** *The variable n is visible only within the doSomething() function. In general, a variable's scope is limited to the function in which it is declared.*

However, there is an easier way: Simply prefix the parameter name with the var keyword to make the parameter a variable:

```
func doSomething(var num: Int) {
    num++
    println(num)
}
```

Note that the parameter duplicates a copy of the argument that is passed in, as the following code snippet shows:

```
num = 8
doSomething(num)    //---prints out 9---
println(num)        //---prints out 8; original value of 8 is unchanged---
```

Any changes made to the variable that is passed to the function remain unchanged after the function has exited.

In-Out Parameters

The previous section showed that a variable passed into a function does not change its value after a function call has returned. This is because the function makes a copy of the variable and all changes are made to the copy.

> **NOTE** When passing value types (such as Int, Double, Float, struct, and String) into a function, the function makes a copy of the variables. However, when passing an instance of a reference type (such as classes), the function references the original instance of the type and does not make a copy. Chapter 8 discusses classes in more detail.

However, sometimes you want a function to change the value of a variable after it has returned. A parameter that persists the changes made within the function is known as an *in-out* parameter. The following shows an example of an in-out parameter:

```
func fullName(inout name:String, withTitle title:String)  {
    name = title + " " + name;
}
```

In the preceding example, the name parameter is prefixed with the inout keyword. This keyword specifies that changes made to the name parameter will be persisted after the function has returned. To see how this works, consider the following code snippet:

```
var myName = "Wei-Meng Lee"
fullName(&myName, withTitle:"Mr.")
println(myName)  //---prints out "Mr. Wei-Meng Lee"---
```

As you can see, the original value of myName was "Wei-Meng Lee". However, after the function has returned, its value has changed to "Mr. Wei-Meng Lee".

Here are the things you need to know when calling a function with `inout` parameters:

> ➤ You need to pass a variable to an `inout` parameter; constants are not allowed.

> ➤ You need to prefix the `&` character before the variable that is passed into an `inout` parameter, to indicate that its value can be changed by the function.

> ➤ In-out parameters cannot have default values.

> ➤ In-out parameters cannot be marked with the `var` or `let` keyword.

FUNCTION TYPES

Every function has a specific function type. To understand this, consider the following two functions:

```
func sum(num1: Int, num2: Int) -> Int {
    return num1 + num2
}

func diff(num1: Int, num2: Int) -> Int {
    return abs(num1 - num2)
}
```

Both functions accept two parameters and return a value of type `Int`. The type of each function is hence `(Int, Int) -> Int`.

> **NOTE** Usually, the type of each function is called the function signature *in programming languages such as Java and C#.*

As another example, the following function has the type `() -> ()`, which you can read as "*a function that does not have any parameters and returns Void*":

```
func doSomething() {
    println("doSomething")
}
```

Defining a Function Type Variable

In Swift, you can define a variable or constant as a function type. For example, you could do the following:

```
var myFunction: (Int, Int) -> Int
```

The preceding statement basically defines a variable called `myFunction` of type "*a function that takes in two* Int *parameters and returns an* Int *value.*" Because `myFunc` has the same function type as the `sum()` function discussed earlier, you can then assign the `sum()` function to it:

```
myFunction = sum
```

You can shorten the preceding statements to:

```
var myFunction: (Int, Int) -> Int = sum
```

Calling a Function Type Variable

You can now call the `sum()` function using the function type variable `myFunction`, like this:

```
println(myFunction(3,4))   //---prints out 7---
```

The `myFunction` variable can be assigned another function that has the `(Int, Int) -> Int` function type:

```
myFunction = diff
```

This time, if you call the `myFunction` again, you will instead be calling the `diff()` function:

```
println(myFunction(3,4))   //---prints out 1---
```

The following table shows the definition of some functions and their corresponding function types.

FUNCTION DEFINITION	FUNCTION TYPE (DESCRIPTION)
```func average(nums: Int...) -> Float {}```	`(Int...) -> Float` The parameter is a variadic parameter; hence, you need to specify the three periods (. . .).
```func joinName(firstName:String, lastName:String, joiner:String = " ") -> String {}```	`(String, String, String) -> String` You need to specify the type for the default parameter (third parameter).
```func doSomething(num1: Int, num2: Int) {}```	`(Int, Int) -> ()` The function does not return a value; hence, you need the `()` in the function type.
```func doSomething() {}```	`() -> ()` The function does not have any parameter and does not return a value; hence, you need to specify the `()` for both parameter and return type.

Returning Function Type in a Function

A function type can be used as the return type of a function. Consider the following example:

```
func chooseFunction(choice:Int) -> (Int, Int)->Int {
    if choice == 0 {
        return sum
    } else {
        return diff
    }
}
```

The `chooseFunction()` function takes in an `Int` parameter and returns a function of type `(Int, Int) -> Int`. In this case, if `choice` is 0, then it returns the `sum()` function; otherwise it returns the `diff()` function.

To use the `chooseFunction()` function, call it and pass in a value and assign its return value to a variable or constant:

```
var functionToUse = chooseFunction(0)
```

The return value can now be called like a function:

```
println(functionToUse(2,6))          //---prints out 8---

functionToUse = chooseFunction(1)
println(functionToUse(2,6))          //---prints out 4---
```

NESTED FUNCTIONS

You can define functions within a function—this is known as *nested functions*. A nested function can only be called within the function in which it is defined.

The `chooseFunction()` function shown in the previous section can be rewritten using nested functions:

```
func chooseFunction(function:Int) -> (Int, Int)->Int {
    func sum(num1: Int, num2: Int) -> Int {
        return num1 + num2
    }

    func diff(num1: Int, num2: Int) -> Int {
        return abs(num1 - num2)
    }

    if function == 0 {
        return sum
    } else {
        return diff
    }
}
```

SUMMARY

In this chapter, you have seen how functions are defined and used. You have also seen the various types of parameters that you can define in your functions and how to call them. Functions play a pivotal role in Swift programming, as they are the cornerstone of object-oriented programming. Chapter 8 discusses how functions are used in classes.

EXERCISES

1. Modify the following code snippet so that it can also return the number of digits divisible by 3:

```
func countNumbers(string: String) -> (odd:Int, even:Int) {
    var odd = 0, even = 0
    for char in string {
        let digit = String(char).toInt()
        if (digit != nil) {
            (digit!) % 2 == 0 ? even++ : odd++
        }
    }
    return (odd, even)
}
```

2. Declare a function so that you can call it like this:

```
doSomething("abc", withSomething: "xyz")
```

3. Write a function that takes in a variable number of Int parameters and returns the sum of all the arguments.

4. Write a variadic function called cat() using default parameters that can be called in the following manner with the outputs shown:

```
println(cat(joiner:":", nums: 1,2,3,4,5,6,7,8,9))
// 1:2:3:4:5:6:7:8:9

println(cat(nums: 1,2,3,4,5))
// 1 2 3 4 5
```

▶ **WHAT YOU LEARNED IN THIS CHAPTER**

TOPIC	KEY CONCEPTS
Defining a function	Use the `func` keyword.
Returning multiple values from a function	Use a tuple to return multiple values from a function.
External parameter names	You can specify an external parameter name to a parameter in a function.
External parameter names shorthand	To use the parameter name as an external parameter name, use the # character.
Default parameter values	You can specify default values for a parameter. For default parameters, you need to specify the parameter name explicitly when calling the function. In addition, for a default parameter, there is no need to specify an external parameter name or use the # shorthand when defining the function, as the default parameter implicitly indicates a named argument.
Variadic parameters	A parameter that accepts a variable number of values is known as a variadic parameter. Note that a variadic parameter must appear last in the parameter list. Also, if you have a function that accepts default parameter values, the variadic parameter must be last in the parameter list.
Constant parameters	By default, all the parameters in a function are constants. To modify the values of parameters, prefix them with the `var` keyword.
In-out parameters	A parameter that persists the changes made within the function is known as an in-out parameter.
Function types	Every function has a specific function type—it specifies the parameters' list and the return type.
Calling a function type variable	You can call a function type variable just like a normal variable.
Returning a function type in a function	You can return a function type from a function.
Nested functions	You can embed functions within a function.

6

Collections

Swift provides two types of collections for storing data of the same type: arrays and dictionaries. An array stores its items in an ordered fashion, whereas a dictionary stores its items in an unordered fashion and uses a unique key to identify each item.

In Swift, both the array and the dictionary are very clear about the type of data they are storing. Unlike the NSArray and NSDictionary classes in Objective-C, arrays and dictionaries in Swift use either type inference or explicit type declaration to ensure that only specific types of data can be stored. This strict rule about data types enables developers to write type-safe code.

ARRAYS

An array is an indexed collection of objects. The following statement shows an array containing three items:

```
var OSes = ["iOS", "Android", "Windows Phone"]
```

In Swift, you create an array using the [] syntax. The compiler automatically infers the type of items inside the array; in this case it is an array of String elements.

In Swift, arrays are implemented internally as structures, not as classes.

Mutability of Arrays

When you declare an array using the var keyword, it is a *mutable array*—meaning the array's size is not fixed and during run time you can add or remove elements from the array. In contrast, if you declare the array using the let keyword, you are creating an immutable array, which means that once the array is created, its element(s) cannot be removed, nor can new elements be added:

```
//---immutable array---
let OSes = ["iOS", "Android", "Windows Phone"]
```

Array Data Types

Note that if you mix the elements of an array with different types, like the following, the compiler will generate an error:

```
var OSes = ["iOS", "Android", "Windows Phone", 25]
```

The compiler will try to infer the data type when the array is being initialized. The fourth element's type is not compatible with the rest of the elements and hence the compilation fails.

In general, most of the time you want your arrays to contain items of the same type, and you can do so explicitly like this:

```
var OSes:Array<String> = ["iOS", "Android", "Windows Phone"]
```

There is a shorthand syntax for arrays whereby you can simply specify the type using the following form: [*DataType*] (where *DataType* is the type of data you want your array to store), like this:

```
var OSes:[String] = ["iOS", "Android", "Windows Phone"]
```

The [String] forces the compiler to check the types of elements inside the array and flag an error when it detects elements of different types.

The following example shows an array of integers:

```
var numbers:[Int] = [0,1,2,3,4,5,6,7,8,9]
```

Retrieving Elements from an Array

To retrieve the items inside an array, use the *subscript syntax*, as follows:

```
var item1 = OSes[0]    // "iOS"
var item2 = OSes[1]    // "Android"
var item3 = OSes[2]    // "Windows Phone"
```

Subscripts enable you to access a specific item of an array directly by writing a value (commonly known as the *index*) in square brackets after the array name. Array indices start at 0, not at 1.

> **NOTE** *The ordering of objects in an array is important, as you access elements inside an array using their position.*

Inserting Elements into an Array

To insert an element into an array at a particular index, use the insert() function:

```
//---inserts a new element into the array at index 2---
OSes.insert("BlackBerry", atIndex: 2)
```

Note that in the preceding function call for insert(), you specify the parameter name - atIndex. This is known as an *external parameter name* and is usually needed if the creator of this function dictates that it needs to be specified.

> **NOTE** *External parameter names are covered in more detail in Chapter 5, "Functions."*

After inserting the element, the array now contains the following elements:

```
[iOS, Android, BlackBerry, Windows Phone]
```

You can insert an element using an index up to the array's size. Figure 6-1 shows that the array size is currently 4, and you can insert an element to the back of the array using the following:

```
OSes.insert("Tizen", atIndex: 4)
```

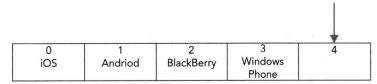

FIGURE 6-1

However, the following statement will result in a runtime failure, as the index of 5 is out of the range (maximum accessible index is 4):

```
//---index out of range---
OSes.insert("Tizen", atIndex: 5)
```

Modifying Elements in an Array

To change the value of an existing item in the array, specify the index of the item and assign a new value to it:

```
OSes[3] = "WinPhone"
```

The array now contains the updated element:

```
[iOS, Android, BlackBerry, WinPhone]
```

Note that you can only modify values of arrays that were declared using the var keyword. If an array is declared using the let keyword, its values are not modifiable.

Appending Elements to an Array

To append an item to an array, use the append() function:

```
OSes.append("Tizen")
```

The array now contains the appended element:

```
[iOS, Android, BlackBerry, WinPhone, Tizen]
```

Alternatively, you can also use the += operator to append to an array:

```
OSes += ["Tizen"]
```

You can also append an array to an existing array:

```
OSes += ["Symbian", "Bada"]
```

The array now contains the appended elements:

```
[iOS, Android, BlackBerry, WinPhone, Tizen, Symbian, Bada]
```

Checking the Size of an Array

To get the length of an array, use the `count` property:

```
var lengthofArray = OSes.count   //---returns 7---
```

To check whether an array is empty, use the `isEmpty()` function:

```
var arrayIsEmpty = OSes.isEmpty
```

Removing Elements from an Array

You can remove elements from an array using the following functions:

```
var os1 = OSes.removeAtIndex(3)     // removes "WinPhone"
var os2 = OSes.removeLast()         // removes "Bada"
OSes.removeAll(keepCapacity: true)  // removes all element
```

Both the `removeAtIndex()` and `removeLast()` functions return the item removed.

For the `removeAll()` function, it clears all elements in the array. If the `keepCapacity` parameter is set to `true`, then the array will maintain its size.

> **NOTE** The `keepCapacity` argument is more for the underlying implementation of the array. Keeping the capacity means that additional elements can be stored later without needing the array to trigger a reallocation of the backing storage.

Iterating over an Array

To iterate over an array, you can use the For-In loop, like this:

```
var OSes = ["iOS", "Android", "Windows Phone"]
for OS in OSes {
    println(OS)
}
```

You can also access specific elements in the array using its indices:

```
var OSes = ["iOS", "Android", "Windows Phone"]
for index in 0...2 {
    println(OSes[index])
}
```

If you need the index and value of each element in the array, you can use the global `enumerate` function to return a tuple for each element in the array:

```
var OSes = ["iOS", "Android", "Windows Phone"]
for (index, value) in enumerate(OSes) {
    println("element \(index) - \(value)")
}
```

The preceding code snippet outputs the following:

```
element 0 - iOS
element 1 - Android
element 2 - Windows Phone
```

Creating an Empty Array

In Swift, you can create an empty array of a specific data type using the initializer syntax, as follows:

```
var names = [String]()
```

The preceding creates an empty array of type `String`. To populate the array, you can use the `append()` method:

```
names.append("Sienna Guillory")
names.append("William Fichtner")
names.append("Hugh Laurie")
names.append("Faye Dunaway")
names.append("Helen Mirren")

for name in names {
    println(name)  //---print out all the names in the array---
}
```

To make `names` an empty array again, assign it to a pair of empty brackets:

```
names = []
```

The following example creates an empty array of type `Int`:

```
var nums = [Int]()
```

You can also create an array of a specific size and initialize each element in the array to a specific value:

```
var scores = [Float](count:5, repeatedValue:0.0)
```

The `count` parameter indicates the size of the array and the `repeatedValue` parameter specifies the initial value for each element in the array. In fact, the preceding statement can also be rewritten without explicitly specifying the type:

```
var scores = Array(count:5, repeatedValue:0.0)
```

The type can be inferred from the argument passed to the `repeatedValue` parameter. If you print out the values for each element in the array as shown here

```
for score in scores {
    println(score)
}
```

you will be able to see initial values for each element:

```
0.0
0.0
0.0
0.0
0.0
```

Testing Arrays for Equality

You can test the equality of two arrays using the `==` operator. Two arrays are equal if they contain exactly the same elements and in exactly the same order. Consider the following example:

```
var array1 = [1,2,3,4,5]
var array2 = [1,2,3,4]
```

These two arrays are not equal, as they do not have the same number of elements:

```
println("Equal: \(array1 == array2)")   //---false---
```

Now append another element to `array2`:

```
array2.append(5)
```

These two arrays are now equal, as they do have the same number of elements in the same exact order:

```
println("Equal: \(array1 == array2)")   //---true---
```

Suppose you have another array:

```
var array3 = [5,1,2,3,4]
```

It is not equal to array1 because the order of the elements is not the same:

```
println("Equal: \(array1 == array3)")   //---false---
```

DICTIONARIES

A dictionary is a collection of objects of the same type that is identified using a key. Consider the following example:

```
var platforms: Dictionary<String, String> = [
    "Apple": "iOS",
    "Google" : "Android",
    "Microsoft" : "Windows Phone"
]
```

Here, `platforms` is a dictionary containing three items. Each item is a key/value pair. For example, `"Apple"` is the key that contains the value `"iOS"`. The declaration specifies that the key and value must both be of the `String` type. Due to type inference, you can shorten the declaration without specifying the `Dictionary` keyword and type specifications:

```
var platforms = [
    "Apple": "iOS",
    "Google" : "Android",
    "Microsoft" : "Windows Phone"
]
```

Unlike arrays, the ordering of items in a dictionary is not important. This is because items are identified by their keys and not their positions. The preceding could also be written like this:

```
var platforms = [
    "Microsoft" : "Windows Phone",
    "Google" : "Android",
    "Apple": "iOS"
]
```

The key of an item in a dictionary is not limited to `String`—it can be any of the *hashable* types (i.e., it must be uniquely representable). The following example shows a dictionary using an integer as its key:

```
var ranking = [
    1: "Gold",
    2: "Silver",
    3: "Bronze"
]
```

The value of an item can itself be another array, as the following example shows:

```
var products = [
    "Apple" : ["iPhone", "iPad", "iPod touch"],
    "Google" : ["Nexus S", "Nexus 4", "Nexus 5"],
    "Microsoft" : ["Lumia 920", "Lumia 1320","Lumia 1520"]
]
```

To access a particular product in the preceding example, you would first specify the key of the item you want to retrieve, followed by the index of the array:

```
println(products["Apple"]![0])   //---iPhone---
println(products["Apple"]![1])   //---iPad---
println(products["Google"]![0])  //---Nexus S---
```

Note that you have to use the ! to force unwrap the value of the dictionary. This is because the dictionary returns you an optional value (it could potentially return you a nil value if you specify a key that does not exist), like this:

```
var models = products["Samsung"]    //---models is nil---
```

The safest way to extract values from a dictionary is to test for nil, like this:

```
var models = products["Apple"]
if models != nil {
    println(models![0])    //---iPhone---
}
```

Mutability of Dictionaries

When creating a dictionary, its mutability (its ability to change its size after it has been created) depends on whether you use either the let or the var keyword. If you use the let keyword, the dictionary is immutable (its size cannot be changed after it has been created), as you are creating a constant. If you use the var keyword, the dictionary is mutable (its size can be changed after its creation), as you are creating a variable.

Retrieving Elements from a Dictionary

To access an item in a dictionary using its subscript, specify its key:

```
var platforms = [
    "Apple": "iOS",
    "Google" : "Android",
    "Microsoft" : "Windows Phone"
]

var ranking = [
    1: "Gold",
    2: "Silver",
    3: "Bronze"
]

println(platforms["Apple"])    //---Optional("iOS")---
println(ranking[2])            //---Optional("Silver")---
```

Because it is possible that the specified key might not exist in the dictionary, the returning result is an *optional* value of the dictionary's value type, which is String? in the first example and Int? in the second.

> **NOTE** *For a discussion on optionals, please refer to Chapter 2, "Data Types."*

You should check whether the value exists before proceeding to work with it:

```
let p = platforms["Apple"]
if p != nil {
    println(p!)    //---iOS---
} else {
    println("Key not found")
}
```

Checking the Size of a Dictionary

To get the number of items within a dictionary, use the `count` property (read-only):

```
var platforms = [
    "Apple": "iOS",
    "Google" : "Android",
    "Microsoft" : "Windows Phone"
]

println(platforms.count)  //---3---
```

Modifying an Item in the Dictionary

To replace the value of an item inside a dictionary, specify its key and assign a new value to it:

```
var platforms = [
    "Apple": "iOS",
    "Google" : "Android",
    "Microsoft" : "Windows Phone"
]

platforms["Microsoft"] = "WinPhone"
```

If the specified key does not already exist in the dictionary, a new item is added. If it already exists, its corresponding value is updated.

Alternatively, you can also use the `updateValue(forKey:)` method and specify the new value for the item as well as its key:

```
platforms.updateValue("WinPhone", forKey: "Microsoft")
```

Note that like arrays, if a dictionary is created using the `let` keyword, you will not be able to modify the value of its members. You can modify the values of a dictionary only if you declare it using the `var` keyword.

Like the previous example, if the key specified does not exist in the dictionary, a new item will be added. However, the `updateValue(forKey:)` method also returns the old value for the specified item if that item already exists. This enables you to check whether the item has been updated. The `updateValue(forKey:)` method returns an *optional* value of the dictionary value type (`String?` in this example). It will contain a string value if the item already exists and `nil` if the specified key is not found (meaning a new item is inserted). You can use this to check whether the item has been updated or newly inserted:

```
if let oldValue = platforms.updateValue("WinPhone", forKey: "Microsoft")
{
    println("The old value for 'Microsoft' was \(oldValue).")
} else {
    println("New key inserted!")
}
```

Removing an Item from the Dictionary

To remove an item from a dictionary, you can simply set it to `nil`:

```
var platforms = [
    "Apple": "iOS",
    "Google" : "Android",
    "Microsoft" : "Windows Phone"
]

platforms["Microsoft"] = nil;
println(platforms.count)        //---2---
```

The number of items inside the dictionary would now be reduced by one.

Alternatively, you can use the `removeValueForKey()` method:

```
if let removedValue = platforms.removeValueForKey("Microsoft") {
    println("Platform removed: \(removedValue)")
} else {
    println("Key not found")
}
```

Like the `updateValue(forKey:)` method discussed in the previous section, the `removeValueForKey()` method returns the value of the key to be removed, and `nil` if the key does not exist.

Iterating over a Dictionary

There are a couple of ways to iterate through a dictionary. First, you can use the For-In loop, like this:

```
var platforms = [
    "Apple": "iOS",
    "Google" : "Android",
    "Microsoft" : "Windows Phone"
```

```
    ]

    for platform in platforms {
        println(platform)
    }
```

The preceding will output the following:

```
(Microsoft, Windows Phone)
(Google, Android)
(Apple, iOS)
```

> **NOTE** *Observe in the preceding output that the values returned from a dictionary might not necessarily follow the order in which they are added.*

You can also specify the key and value separately:

```
    for (company, platform) in platforms {
        println("\(company) - \(platform)")
    }
```

The preceding will output the following:

```
Microsoft - Windows Phone
Google - Android
Apple - iOS
```

You can also use the For-In loop to iterate through the keys inside a dictionary using the keys property:

```
    for company in platforms.keys {
        println("Company - \(company)")
    }
```

The preceding code snippet will output the following:

```
Company - Microsoft
Company - Google
Company - Apple
```

The following example iterates through the values in a dictionary using the values property:

```
    for platform in platforms.values {
        println("Platform - \(platform)")
    }
```

The preceding code snippet will output the following:

```
Platform - Windows Phone
Platform - Android
Platform - iOS
```

You can also assign the keys or values of a dictionary directly to an array:

```
let companies = platforms.keys
let oses = platforms.values
```

Creating an Empty Dictionary

In Swift, you can create an empty dictionary of a specific data type using the initializer syntax, like this:

```
var months = Dictionary<Int, String>()
```

The preceding example creates an empty dictionary of `Int` key type and `String` value type.

To populate the dictionary, specify the key and its corresponding value:

```
months[1]  = "January"
months[2]  = "February"
months[3]  = "March"
months[4]  = "April"
months[5]  = "May"
months[6]  = "June"
months[7]  = "July"
months[8]  = "August"
months[9]  = "September"
months[10] = "October"
months[11] = "November"
months[12] = "December"
```

To make `months` an empty dictionary again, assign it to a pair of brackets with a colon within it:

```
months = [:]
```

Testing Dictionaries for Equality

You can test the equality of two dictionaries using the `==` operator. Two dictionaries are equal if they contain exactly the same keys and values, as the following illustrates:

```
var dic1 = [
    "1": "a",
    "2": "b",
    "3": "c",
]

var dic2 = [
    "3": "c",
    "1": "a",
]

println("Equal: \(dic1 == dic2)")  //---false---
```

The preceding expression evaluates to `false`, as the two dictionaries do not contain the same exact number of keys and values. However, if you add a new item to `dic2`, then it will evaluate to `true`:

```
dic2["2"] = "b"
println("Equal: \(dic1 == dic2)")  //---true---
```

COPYING THE BEHAVIOR OF ARRAYS AND DICTIONARIES

You can copy an array by assigning it to another variable or constant, like this:

```
var array1 = [1,2,3,4,5]
var array2 = array1
```

In the preceding example, `array1` is assigned to another variable `array2`. In Swift, when you assign an array to another variable, a copy of the original array is duplicated and assigned to the second array, as shown in Figure 6-2.

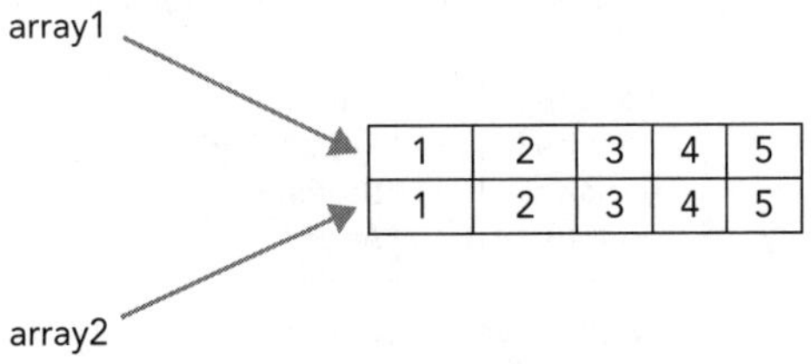

FIGURE 6-2

To prove this, you can make some changes to `array1` and then output the content of both arrays, like this:

```
array1[1] = 20
println(array1)  //---[1,20,3,4,5]---
println(array2)  //---[1,2,3,4,5]---
```

As evident in the result, a change to `array1`'s element only affects itself.

For dictionaries, copying behavior is similar—a copy of the dictionary is created and assigned to the second variable. Consider the following example dictionary:

```
var colors = [
    1 : "Red",
    2 : "Green",
    3 : "Blue"
]
```

The following statement copies the dictionary to another one:

```
var copyOfColors = colors
```

Make a change to the `colors` dictionary

```
colors[1] = "Yellow"
```

and print the values for both dictionaries:

```
for color in colors {
    println(color)
```

```
    }

for color in copyOfColors {
    println(color)
}
```

You will see that `colors` now contains the following items

```
(1, Yellow)
(2, Green)
(3, Blue)
```

and `copyOfColors` contains the original list of items:

```
(1, Red)
(2, Green)
(3, Blue)
```

SUMMARY

In this chapter, you learned about the two collection types in Swift: arrays and dictionaries. Both arrays and dictionaries contain items of the same type. The fundamental difference between an array and a dictionary is the way items are stored and retrieved. For arrays, the order in which items are added is important, as it affects the positioning of items and hence how they are retrieved. For dictionaries, items are identified using a unique key, which provides a lot more flexibility when it comes to adding and retrieving items.

EXERCISES

1. Create an array of integers and output all the odd numbers contained within it.

2. Create a dictionary to store a user's info, such as username, password, and date of birth.

3. Given the following code snippet:

```
var products = [
    "Apple" : ["iPhone", "iPad", "iPod touch"],
    "Google" : ["Nexus S", "Nexus 4", "Nexus 5"],
    "Microsoft" : ["Lumia 920", "Lumia 1320","Lumia 1520"]
]
```

Write the code to print out the following:

```
Microsoft
========
Lumia 920
Lumia 1320
Lumia 1520

Apple
========
```

```
iPhone
iPad
iPod touch

Google
========
Nexus S
Nexus 4
Nexus 5
```

► **WHAT YOU LEARNED IN THIS CHAPTER**

TOPIC	KEY CONCEPTS
Creating an array	You create an array using the [*type*] syntax.
Mutability of arrays	Arrays are immutable if they are created with the `let` keyword; they are mutable only if they are created with the `var` keyword.
Retrieving elements from an array	You can use the subscript syntax to access an individual element of an array.
Inserting an element into an array	Use the `insert()` function to insert an element into an array.
Appending an element to an array	Use the `append()` function, or you can directly add an array to another array using the `+=` operator.
Checking the size of an array	Use the `count` property.
Removing an element from an array	Use the `removeAtIndex()`, `removeLast()`, or `removeAll()` function.
Iterating over an array	Use the For-In loop.
Testing array equality	Use the `==` operator.
Creating a dictionary	You create a dictionary using the `Dictionary[`*type*`, `*type*`]` syntax.
Retrieving the elements from a dictionary	Specify the key of the items in a dictionary; values from a dictionary are of optional type.
Mutability of dictionaries	Dictionaries are immutable if they are created with the `let` keyword; they are mutable only if they are created with the `var` keyword.
Size of a dictionary	Use the `count` property.
Modifying elements in a dictionary	Specify the key of the item and assign it the new value.
Removing an element in a dictionary	Specify the key of the item and set it to `nil`.
Iterating over a dictionary	Use the For-In loop.
Testing dictionaries for equality	Use the `==` operator.
Copy behaviors of arrays and dictionaries	When an array or dictionary is copied, a copy is made and assigned to the variable.

7

Control Flow and Looping

One of the most important aspects of a programming language is its ability to make decisions and perform repetitive tasks. In this aspect, Swift provides the usual flow control statements for making decisions through the use of the If-Else statement. For making multiple comparisons, Swift provides the Switch statement, which in addition to being similar to its counterpart in C, is much more powerful and flexible.

Swift also supports the C-style For and While loops and introduces the new For-In loop to iterate through arrays, dictionaries, and strings.

FLOW CONTROL

Swift primarily provides two types of statements for flow control: the If statement and the Switch statement.

If you have programmed before, you are familiar with the If statement. The If statement enables you to make a decision based on a certain condition(s). If the condition(s) are met, the block of statement enclosed by the If statement would be executed. If you need to make a decision based on several conditions, you could use the more efficient Switch statement, which enables you to specify the conditions without using multiple If statements.

If Statement

Swift supports the traditional C-style If statement construct for decision-making. The syntax for the If statement is as follows:

```
if condition {
    statement(s)
}
```

Here is an example of the If statement:

```
var raining = true  //---raining is of type Boolean---
if raining {
    println("Raining now")
}
```

> **NOTE** In Swift, there is no need to enclose the condition within a pair of parentheses (()).

In the preceding code snippet, as `raining` is a `Bool` value, you can simply specify the variable name in the condition. The preceding example will output the following:

```
Raining now
```

You can also explicitly perform the comparison using a comparison operator:

```
if raining == true {
    println("Raining now")
}
```

In C/C++, non-zero values are considered `true` and are often used in the If statement. Consider the following code snippet in C:

```
//---in C/C++---
Int number = 1
if (number) {
    //---number is non-zero---
}
```

In the preceding example, `number` is non-zero (it has a value of 1) and hence the condition evaluates to `true`. In Swift, for non-Boolean variables (or constants) you are not allowed to specify the condition without an explicit logical comparison:

```
var number = 1  //---number is of Int type---
if number {     //---this is not allowed in Swift---
    println("Number is non-zero")
}
```

To perform the comparison, you need to explicitly specify the comparison operator:

```
if number == 1 {
    println("Number is non-zero")
}
```

Also commonly performed in C/C++ is the use of the assignment operator within the condition:

```
//---in C/C++---
if (number=5) { //---number is non-zero---

}
```

> **NOTE** Using the assignment operator (=) within a condition is a major source of bugs in C programs. Programmers often intend to use the comparison operator (==) but mistakenly use the assignment operator; and so long as they assign a non-zero value, the condition always evaluates to `true`.

In the preceding statement, the value 5 is assigned to `number`; and because the number is now non-zero, the condition evaluates to `true` and hence the block in the If statement is executed. In Swift, this is not allowed:

```
if number = 5 { //---not allowed in Swift---
    println("Number is non-zero")
}
```

This limitation is useful in preventing unintended actions on the developer's part.

If-Else Statement

An extension of the If statement is the If-Else statement. The If-Else statement has the following syntax:

```
if condition {
    statement(s)
```

```
} else {
    statement(s)
}
```

Any statements enclosed by the Else block are executed when the condition evaluates to `false`. Here is an example:

```
var temperatureInCelsius = 25
if (temperatureInCelsius>30) {
    println("This is hot!")
} else {
    println("This is cooling!")
}
```

The preceding code snippet checks the temperature (in Celsius) and outputs the statement "This is hot!" if it more than 30 degrees Celsius. If it is less than or equal to 30 degrees Celsius, it outputs the statement "This is cooling!" The preceding example will output the following:

```
This is cooling!
```

The Else block can also be another If-Else block, as the following example illustrates:

```
var temperatureInCelsius = 0
if temperatureInCelsius>30 {
    println("This is hot!")
} else if temperatureInCelsius>0 {
    println("This is cooling!")
} else {
    println("This is freezing!")
}
```

The preceding code will output the following statement:

```
This is freezing!
```

Switch Statement

Very often, you will need to perform a number of If-Else statements. Consider the case where you have an integer representing the day of the week. For example, one represents Monday, two represents Tuesday, and so on. If you were to use the If-Else statement, that would be too cumbersome and makes the code unwieldy. For this purpose, you should use the *Switch* statement. The Switch statement has the following syntax:

```
switch variable/constant {
    case value_1:
        statement(s)
    case value_2:
        statement(s)
    ...

        ...
    case value_n:
        statement(s)
```

```
    default:
        statement(s)
}
```

The value of the variable/constant is used for comparison with the various values specified (*value_1*, *value2*, . . ., *value_n*). If a match occurs, any statements following the value are executed (specified using the `case` keyword). If no match is found, any statements specified after the `default` keyword are executed.

> **NOTE** *Unlike C and Objective-C (as well as other programming languages), there is no need to specify a Break statement after the last statement in each case. Immediately after any statements in a case block are executed, the Switch statement finishes its execution. In C, a Break statement is needed to prevent the statements after the current case from execution. This behavior is known as implicit fallthrough. In Swift, there is no implicit fallthrough—once the statements in a case are executed, the Switch statement ends.*

Every Switch statement must be exhaustive. In other words, the value that you are trying to match must be matched by one of the various cases in the Switch statement. As it is sometimes not feasible to list all the cases, you would need to use the `default` case to match the remaining unmatched cases.

Matching Numbers

A common use of the Switch statement is for matching numbers. The following code snippet shows how to use the Switch statement to convert a number to the day of week:

```
var day = 6
var dayOfWeek: String
switch day {
    case 1:
        dayOfWeek = "Monday"
    case 2:
        dayOfWeek = "Tuesday"
    case 3:
        dayOfWeek = "Wednesday"
    case 4:
        dayOfWeek = "Thursday"
    case 5:
        dayOfWeek = "Friday"
    case 6:
        dayOfWeek = "Saturday"
    case 7:
        dayOfWeek = "Sunday"
    default:
        dayOfWeek = ""
}
println(dayOfWeek) //---prints Saturday---
```

If day contains a number other than a number from 1 to 7, the default case will match and the dayOfWeek variable will be set to an empty string.

Matching Characters

You can also use the Switch statement to match characters, as the following code snippet demonstrates:

```
var grade: Character
grade = "A"
switch grade {
    case "A", "B", "C", "D":
        println("Passed")
    case "F":
        println("Failed")
    default:
        println("Undefined")
}
```

The first case checks whether grade contains the character "A," "B," "C," or "D." The second case tries to match the character "F." If all fails, the default case is matched.

Fallthrough

As mentioned earlier, Swift does not support fallthrough in the Switch statement. If you are familiar with C/C++, you would be tempted to do the following:

```
var grade: Character
grade = "B"
switch grade {
    case "A":
    case "B":
    case "C":
    case "D":
        println("Passed")
    case "F":
        println("Failed")
    default:
        println("Undefined")
}
```

This is not allowed in Swift. In Swift, each case must have at least one executable statement (comments are not executable statements). If you want to implement the fallthrough behavior in Swift, you need to explicitly use the fallthrough keyword:

```
var grade: Character
grade = "A"
switch grade {
    case "A":
        fallthrough
    case "B":
        fallthrough
```

```
        case "C":
            fallthrough
        case "D":
            println("Passed")
        case "F":
            println("Failed")
        default:
            println("Undefined")
    }
```

In this case, after matching the first case ("A"), the execution will fallthrough to the next case ("B"), which will then fallthrough to the next case ("C"), and finally the next case ("D"). The Switch statement ends after outputting the line "Passed."

Fallthroughs are sometimes useful. Suppose you want to not only output a pass or fail message after checking the grade, but also output a more detailed message depending on the grade. You could do the following:

```
var grade: Character
grade = "A"
switch grade {
    case "A":
        print("Excellent! ")
        fallthrough
    case "B":
        print("Well done! ")
        fallthrough
    case "C":
        print("Good! ")
        fallthrough
    case "D":
        println("You have passed.")
    case "F":
        println("Failed")
    default:
        println("Undefined")
}
```

If grade is "A," the output message would be as follows:

```
Excellent! Well done! Good! You have passed.
```

If grade is "B," the output message would instead be this:

```
Well done! Good! You have passed.
```

Matching a Range of Numbers

You can also perform range matching using the Switch statement. The following code snippet shows how you can match a range of numbers against a variable/constant:

```
var percentage = 85
switch percentage {
```

```
        case 0...20:
            println("Group 1")
        case 21...40:
            println("Group 2")
        case 41...60:
            println("Group 3")
        case 61...80:
            println("Group 4")
        case 81...100:
            println("Group 5")
        default:
            println("Invalid percentage")
    }
```

The preceding code snippet outputs the following line:

```
Group 5
```

> **NOTE** *The range of numbers that you are matching need not be integers. You can also specify floating-point numbers.*

The closed ranged operator (represented by …) specifies the range of numbers that you are comparing.

Matching Tuples

The Switch statement also works with *tuples*, an ordered set of numbers. Suppose you have the following tuples:

```
//---(math, science)---
var scores = (70,40)
```

The `scores` tuple stores the score for the math and science examinations, respectively. You can use the Switch statement to check the scores for each subject simultaneously. Consider the following example:

```
switch scores {
    case (0,0):
        println("This is not good!")
    case (100,100):
        println("Perfect scores!")
    case (50...100, _):
        println("Math passed!")
    case (_, 50...100):
        println("Science passed!")
    default:
        println("Both failed!")
}
```

In this case, if the scores for both subjects are 0, the first case will match ((0,0)). If both scores are 100, the second case will match ((100,100)). The third case ((50...100, _)) will only match the score for the math subject—if it is between 50 and 100. The underscore (_) matches any value for the second subject (science). The fourth case matches any value for the math subject and checks to see if the science subject is between 50 and 100.

If the score is (70, 40), the statement "Math pass!" will be output. If the score is (40, 88), the statement "Science pass!" will be output. If the score is (30, 20), the statement "Both failed" will be output.

> **NOTE** In Swift, you are allowed to have overlapping cases. In other words, you might have more than one match with the different cases. The first matching case will always be executed.

Value Bindings

In the previous section, you have two cases in which you try to match the score of one subject and ignore another:

```
case (50...100, _):    //---ignore science---
case (_, 50...100):    //---ignore math---
```

But what if after matching the score of one subject you also want to get the score of the other? In Swift, the Switch statement allows you to bind the value(s) its matches to temporary variables or constants. This is known as *value-binding*.

The example used in the previous section can be modified to demonstrate value-binding:

```
//---(math, science)---
var scores = (70,60)
switch scores {
    case (0,0):
        println("This is not good!")
    case (100,100):
        println("Perfect score!")
    case (50...100, let science):
        println("Math passed!")
        if science<50 {
            println("But Science failed!")
        } else {
            println("And Science passed too!")
        }
    case (let math, 50...100):
        println("Science passed!")
        if math<50 {
            println("But Math failed!")
        } else {
            println("And Math passed too!")
        }
    default:
        println("Both failed!")
}
```

> **NOTE** In the preceding example, `science` and `math` are declared as constants using the `let` keyword. However, you could also declare them as variables using the `var` keyword. If they were declared as variables, all changes made would only have an effect within the body of the case.

In the third case statement, after matching the score for the math subject, you assign the score of the science subject to the `science` constant (as indicated using the `let` keyword):

```
case (50...100, let science):
    println("Math passed!")
    if science<50 {
        println("But Science failed!")
    } else {
        println("And Science passed too!")
    }
```

You can then use the `science` variable to determine its passing status.

Likewise, you do the same to the fourth case statement:

```
case (let math, 50...100):
    println("Science passed!")
    if math<50 {
        println("But Math failed!")
    } else {
        println("And Math passed too!")
    }
```

You can also remove the default case and replace it with a case that matches *any* values:

```
//---(math, science)---
var scores = (30,20)
switch scores {
    case (0,0):
        println("This is not good!")
    case (100,100):
        println("Perfect score!")
    case (50...100, let science):
        println("Math passed!")
        if science<50 {
            println("But Science failed!")
        } else {
            println("And Science passed too!")
        }
    case (let math, 50...100):
        println("Science passed!")
        if math<50 {
            println("But Math failed!")
        } else {
            println("And Math passed too!")
        }
```

```
    /*
    default:
        println("Both failed!")
    */
    case (let math, let science):
        println("Math is \(math) and Science is \(science)")
}
```

The preceding code snippet will output the following:

```
Math is 30 and Science is 20
```

Instead of writing the let keyword twice for both variables as

```
case (let math, let science):
```

you could rewrite it like this:

```
case let (math, science):
    println("Math is \(math) and Science is \(science)")
```

Where Clause

You can use the Switch statement together with a *where* clause to check for additional conditions. For example, if you wanted to check if the scores for both subjects are greater than 80, you could write the following case:

```
//---(math, science)---
var scores = (90,90)
switch scores {
    case (0,0):
        println("This is not good!")
    case (100,100):
        println("Perfect score!")
    case let (math, science) where math > 80 && science > 80:
        println("Well done!")
    case (50...100, let science):
        println("Math pass!")
        if science<50 {
            println("But Science fail!")
        } else {
            println("And Science also pass!")
        }
    case (let math, 50...100):
        println("Science pass!")
        if math<50 {
            println("But Math fail!")
        } else {
            println("And Math also pass!")
        }
    case let (math, science):
        println("Math is \(math) and Science is \(science)")
}
```

In the preceding code snippet, the third case assigns the scores of the math and science subjects to the temporary variables `math` and `science`, respectively, and uses the `where` clause to specify the condition that the scores for both math and science must be greater than 80. The preceding example will output the following statement:

```
Well done!
```

If you want to match the case where the math score is greater than the science score, you can specify the following `where` clause:

```
case let (math, science) where math > science:
    println("You have done well for Math!")
```

LOOPING

The capability to repeatedly execute statements is one of the most useful features of a programming language. Swift supports the following loop statements:

➤ For-In

➤ For

➤ While

➤ Do-While

For-In Loop

Swift supports a new loop statement known as the For-In loop. The For-In loop iterates over a collection of items (such as an array or a dictionary) as well as a range of numbers.

The following code snippet prints out the numbers from 0 to 9 using the For-In loop:

```
for i in 0...9 {
    println(i)
}
```

The closed ranged operator (represented by . . .) defines a range of numbers from 0 to 9 (inclusive). The `i` is a constant whose value is initially set to 0 for the first iteration. After executing the statement(s) in the For-In loop (as defined by the {}), the value of `i` is incremented to 1, and so on. Because `i` is a constant, you are not allowed to modify its value within the loop, like this:

```
for i in 0...9 {
    i++    //---this is not allowed as i is a constant---
    println(i)
}
```

You can also use the For-In loop to output characters in Unicode, like the following:

```
for c in 65 ... 90 {
    println(Character(UnicodeScalar(c)))   //---prints out 'A' to 'Z'---
}
```

The `UnicodeScaler` is a structure that takes in an initializer containing the number representing a character in Unicode. You then convert it to a `Character` type.

You can nest a For-In loop within another For-In loop:

```
//---Nested Loop---
for i in 1...10{
    for j in 1...10 {
        println("\(i) x \(j) = \(i*j)")
    }
    println("=============")
}
```

The preceding code snippet outputs the times table from 1 to 10:

```
1 x 1 = 1
1 x 2 = 2
1 x 3 = 3
1 x 4 = 4
1 x 5 = 5
1 x 6 = 6
1 x 7 = 7
1 x 8 = 8
1 x 9 = 9
1 x 10 = 10
=============
2 x 1 = 2
2 x 2 = 4
2 x 3 = 6
2 x 4 = 8
2 x 5 = 10
2 x 6 = 12
2 x 7 = 14
2 x 8 = 16
2 x 9 = 18
2 x 10 = 20
=============
3 x 1 = 3
3 x 2 = 6
3 x 3 = 9
...
```

If you simply want to perform an action a fixed number of times and don't care about the number of each iteration, you can simply specify an underscore (_) in place of a constant:

```
//---print * 5 times---
for _ in 1...5 {
    print("*")   //---prints out ****---
}
```

The preceding code snippet outputs the asterisk five times.

The For-In loop also works with arrays, as shown here:

```
var fruits = ["apple", "pineapple", "orange", "durian", "guava"]
for f in fruits {
    println(f)
}
```

The preceding example iterates through the five elements contained within the `fruits` array and outputs them:

```
apple
pineapple
orange
durian
guava
```

You can also iterate through a dictionary, as the following example shows:

```
var courses = [
    "IOS101": "Foundation of iPhone Programming",
    "AND101": "Foundation of Android Programming",
    "WNP101": "Foundation of Windows Phone Programming"
]

for (id, title) in courses {
    println("\(id) - \(title)")
}
```

The preceding code outputs the following:

```
IOS101 - Foundation of iPhone Programming
AND101 - Foundation of Android Programming
WNP101 - Foundation of Windows Phone Programming
```

You can also iterate through a string and extract each character, as the following shows:

```
var str = "Swift Programming"
for c in str {
    println(c)
}
```

In the preceding code, c is assigned to each of the characters in the string during each iteration of the loop. It outputs the following:

```
S
w
i
f
t

P
r
o
g
r
a
m
m
i
n
g
```

Traditional For Loop

Swift also supports the traditional For loop in C, using the following syntax:

```
for initialization; condition; increment/decrement {
    statement(s)
}
```

> **NOTE** *Unlike traditional C, in Swift you do not need to enclose the* initialization; condition; increment/decrement *block using a pair of parentheses (()).*

The following code snippet outputs the numbers from 0 to 4:

```
//---print from 0 to 4---
for var i = 0; i<5; i++ {
    println(i)
}
```

> **NOTE** *The initializer must be a variable, not a constant, as its value needs to change during the iteration of the loop.*

When the loop starts, i is initialized to 0, and its value is checked to see if it is less than five. If it evaluates to true, the value of i is output. If it evaluates to false, the For loop will end. After all the statements in a For loop have been executed, the value of i is incremented by one. It is then checked if it is less than five, and the loop continues if it evaluates to true.

Note that the i variable is not accessible after the loop exits, as it is defined within the For loop construct:

```
//---print from 0 to 4---
for var i = 0; i<5; i++ {
    println(i)
}
println(i)   //---i is not defined---
```

If you want i to be visible after the loop, create it first, before using it in the loop:

```
//---print from 0 to 4---
var i:Int
for i = 0; i<5; i++ {
    println(i)
}
println(i)   //--5---
```

When you define i without initializing it with a value, you need to specify its type. The preceding can also be rewritten by initializing the value of i and then omitting the initialization in the For loop:

```
//---print from 0 to 4---
var i = 0
for ; i<5; i++ {   //---the initialization part can be omitted---
    println(i)
}
println(i)    //-5---
```

You can also count downwards—the following code snippet outputs the numbers from 5 to 1:

```
//---print from 5 to 1---
for var i = 5; i>0; i--- {
    println(i)
}
```

You can use the enumerate() function in Swift to iterate over an array. The enumerate() function returns a tuple containing the index and the value of each element in the array:

```
let names = ["Mary", "Chloe", "Margaret", "Ryan"]
for (index, value) in enumerate(names) {
    println("names[\(index)] - \(value)")
}
```

The preceding code snippet outputs the following:

```
names[0]  - Mary
names[1]  - Chloe
names[2]  - Margaret
names[3]  - Ryan
```

While Loop

In addition to the For loop, Swift also provides the While loop. The While loop executes a block of statements repeatedly as long as the specified condition is true:

```
while condition {
    statement(s)
}
```

The following code snippet outputs the series of numbers 0 to 4:

```
var index = 0
while index<5 {
    println(index++)
}
```

Before the first iteration starts, the While loop checks the value of index. If it is less than 5, it will enter the loop and execute the statement(s) within. Within the block, you increment the value of index after outputting it to the screen. The condition is then checked again to see it is evaluates to true. As long as it evaluates to `true`, the loop is repeated. When `index` finally becomes 5, the While loop ends.

The For loop introduced in the previous section is ideal for situations in which you are iterating over a set of items (such as an array or a dictionary) or when you know beforehand how many iterations you need to execute a certain block of code. For situations in which it isn't very clear how many times you need to execute a block of code, the While loop may be more applicable.

Consider the problem of determining how many times a number is divisible by two. For example, the number of times 4 is divisible by 2 is 2:

> 4/2 = 2 (1 time)
>
> 2/2 = 1 (2 times)

Consider another example: the number of times 14 is divisible by 2 is 3:

> 14/2 = 7 (1 time)
>
> 7/2 = 3 (2 times)
>
> 3/2 = 1 (3 times)

In this scenario, you can use a loop to calculate the number of times the number is divisible by 2— keep dividing the number as long as the number is greater than 1. However, because you are not sure how many times your loop needs to iterate until the number is 1, it would be better and more elegant to use a While loop. The preceding problem could be solved using the following code snippet:

```
var counter = 0
var num = 32
while num > 1 {
    counter++
    num /= 2
}
println("The number is \(counter) times divisible by 2")
```

The preceding will output the following:

```
The number is 5 times divisible by 2
```

Do-While Loop

A variation of the While loop is the Do-While loop. The Do-While loop has the following syntax:

```
do {
    statement(s)
} while condition
```

The following code snippet outputs the series of numbers from 0 to 4:

```
index = 0
do {
    println(index++)
} while (index<5)
```

The Do-While executes the block of statement(s) enclosed by the pair of braces ({}) first, before checking the condition to decide if the looping will continue. If the condition evaluates to `true`, the loop continues. If it evaluates to `false`, then the loop exits.

> **NOTE** The key difference between the While loop and the Do-While loop is that the statements within a Do-While loop execute at least once, since their condition is evaluated at the end of the block.

Control Transfer Statements

So far you have seen the use of the For and While loops for executing code repeatedly. As long as the condition specified in the loop evaluates to `true`, the block of code is executed. Sometimes you want to have the capability to alter the order in which the code is executed. You can do so using the Break or Continue *control transfer statements*.

Break Statement

Consider the following scenario: You have a string of characters and you want to find the index of the first occurrence of a character. For example, in the string "This is a string," the index of the character "a" is 8. You could solve this problem using the following code snippet:

```
var c:Character
var found = false
var index = 0
for c in "This is a string" {
    if c != "a" && !found {
        index++
    } else {
        found = true
    }
}
println("Position of 'a' is \(index)")
```

In the preceding code, you iterate through the entire string and examine each character. If the character is not what you are looking for, increment the index and continue searching. Once you have found the character, you set the `found` Boolean variable to `true` and the index will no longer be incremented. The downside to this code snippet is that you are going through each character until the end of the string, even if you have already found the one for which you are looking. An improved version looks like this, using the Break statement:

```
var c:Character
var index = 0
for c in "This is a string" {
    if c == "a" {
        break
    }
    index++
}
println("Position of 'a' is \(index)")
```

Here, you use the Break statement to end the loop the moment the character you are looking for is found. This is much more efficient than the earlier solution. When you use the Break statement within a loop (such as a For, While, or Do-While loop), the control is transferred to the first line of code after the closing brace (}).

The Break statement is also useful in the Switch statement. Recall the following Switch statement that you saw earlier in this chapter:

```
var percentage = 85
switch percentage {
    case 0...20:
        println("Group 1")
    case 21...40:
        println("Group 2")
    case 41...60:
        println("Group 3")
    case 61...80:
        println("Group 4")
    case 81...100:
        println("Group 5")
    default:
        println("Invalid percentage")
}
```

Oftentimes, you may not need to do anything for a certain case; in this example, for instance, you might not need to output anything should the percentage fall outside the range of 0 to 100. However, you cannot simply leave the case statement empty, like this:

```
var percentage = 85
switch percentage {
    case 0...20:
        println("Group 1")
    case 21...40:
        println("Group 2")
    case 41...60:
        println("Group 3")
    case 61...80:
        println("Group 4")
    case 81...100:
        println("Group 5")
    default:
        //---each case must have an executable statement
        // comments like this do not count as executable statement---
}
```

As each case in a Switch statement must have at least an executable statement, you can use a Break statement, like this:

```
var percentage = 85
switch percentage {
    case 0...20:
        println("Group 1")
    case 21...40:
        println("Group 2")
```

```
        case 41...60:
            println("Group 3")
        case 61...80:
            println("Group 4")
        case 81...100:
            println("Group 5")
        default:
            break
    }
```

The preceding Break statement will end the execution of the Switch statement.

Continue Statement

Another control transfer statement that you can use in your loop is Continue. The Continue statement basically says *"stop the execution of the rest of the statements in this loop and go on to the next iteration."*

Consider the scenario in which you want to count the number of characters in a string, excluding the spaces. The following snippet shows how this could be done with the Continue statement:

```
//---count the number of characters (excluding spaces)---
var c:Character
var count = 0
for c in "This is a string" {
    if c == " " {
        continue
    }
    count++
}
println("Number of characters is \(count)")
```

In the preceding code snippet, when a space is encountered, the Continue statement transfers the execution to the next iteration of the loop, effectively bypassing the statement where the count variable is incremented. The preceding code snippet will output the following:

```
Number of characters is 13
```

Labeled Statement

Although the Break or Continue statement enables you to exit from a loop and continue on to the next iteration of a loop, things are a little more complex when you have a nested loop. Consider the following example:

```
var i = 0
while i<3 {
    i++
    var j = 0
    while j<3 {
        j++
        println("(\(i),\(j))")
    }
}
```

The preceding code snippet has two While loops—one nested within another. It outputs the following lines:

```
(1,1)
(1,2)
(1,3)
(2,1)
(2,2)
(2,3)
(3,1)
(3,2)
(3,3)
```

What happens if within the inner loop you execute a break, as shown here:

```
var i = 0
while i<3 {
    i++
    var j = 0
    while j<3 {
        j++
        println("(\(i),\(j))")
        break
    }
}
```

In this case, the compiler will assume that you are trying to exit from the inner loop, and thus the preceding code will output the following:

```
(1,1)
(2,1)
(3,1)
```

What if you actually wanted to break from the outer loop? In this case, you can add a label prior to the outer While loop:

```
var i = 0
outerLoop: while i<3 {
    i++
    var j = 0
    while j<3 {
        j++
        println("(\(i),\(j))")
        break outerLoop  //---exit the inner While loop---
    }
}
```

You can explicitly specify which While loop you are trying to break out of by specifying the label (outerLoop). The preceding code outputs this line:

```
(1,1)
```

You can also use the labeled statement with the `continue` keyword:

```
var i = 0
outerLoop: while i<3 {
    i++
    var j = 0
    while j<3 {
        j++
        println("(\(i),\(j))")
        continue outerLoop  //---go to the next iteration of the
                            // outer While loop---
    }
}
```

The preceding code outputs the following lines:

```
(1,1)
(2,1)
(3,1)
```

SUMMARY

This chapter demonstrated how to make decisions using the If-Else and Switch statements. As you have seen, Swift has made the Switch statement much more powerful in comparison to its C counterpart. In addition, you have also seen how to perform looping using the For loop, the While loop, and the Do-While loop.

EXERCISES

1. The Fibonacci numbers is a series of numbers in the following sequence:

   ```
   1,1,2,3,5,8,13,21,34,55,89,144,...
   ```

   Write the code snippet to print out the Fibonacci sequence.

2. In mathematics, GCD (greatest common divisor) of two or more integers is that largest positive number that can divide the numbers without a remainder. For example, the GCD of 8 and 12 is 4. Write a function in Swift to compute the GCD of two integers.

3. A prime number is a natural number greater than 1 that has no positive divisors other than 1 and itself. Write a function in Swift to output the list of prime numbers from 2 to 1000:

```
2 is prime
3 is prime
5 is prime
7 is prime
11 is prime
13 is prime
17 is prime
19 is prime
23 is prime
29 is prime
31 is prime
37 is prime
41 is prime
. . .
```

▶ WHAT YOU LEARNED IN THIS CHAPTER

TOPIC	KEY CONCEPTS
Making decisions	Use the If-Else statement.
Making multiple decisions	Use the Switch statement.
Fallthroughs	By default, Swift does not support fallthroughs; however, you can explicitly initiate a fallthrough by using the `fallthough` keyword.
Types of loops	For-In, For, While, and Do-While.
Control transfer statements	Use the Break statement to break out of a loop. Use the Continue statement to immediately continue to the next iteration of the loop.
Labeled statements	Allow you to specifically indicate which loop you want to break out/continue with.

8

Structures and Classes

WHAT YOU WILL LEARN IN THIS CHAPTER:

➤ How to define a structure

➤ How to create an instance of a structure

➤ How to initialize a structure's properties

➤ How to compare two structures

➤ How to define a class

➤ How to define properties within a class

➤ The different types of properties

➤ How to create initializers for a class

➤ How to compare instances of a class

➤ How to define methods in a class

Object-oriented programming (OOP) is one of the most important features in Swift programming—and structures and classes play an important role in supporting that. In Swift, structures and classes share many similarities, and many concepts that apply to classes apply to structure as well.

In this chapter, you will learn how to define structures and classes, and then use them. You will learn how to define the different types of properties in structures and classes, as well as define methods. By the end of this chapter, you will have a solid understanding of how structures and classes work in Swift.

STRUCTURES

A *structure* is a special kind of data type that groups a list of variables and places them under a unified name. The group of variables contained within a structure may have diverse data types. Structures are useful for storing related group of data. For example, consider a scenario in which you are implementing a game of Go. Figure 8-1 shows the board layout of Go. A typical game of Go has a grid of 19 × 19 lines, and players place markers, referred to as stones, on the intersections of these lines. To represent a stone on the Go board, you can use a structure containing two variables: row and column.

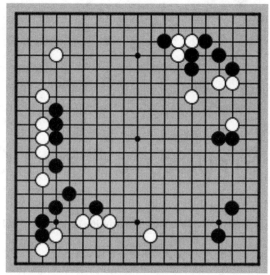

FIGURE 8-1

The following code snippet defines the structure named Go:

```
struct Go {
    var row = 0       //---0...18---
    var column = 0    //---0...18---
}
```

For structure names, the recommendation is to use UpperCamelCase (such as CustomerAddress, EmployeeCredential, etc.).

The Go structure has two properties called row and column, which are both initialized to 0 (their default values). To create an instance of the Go structure, use the structure's default initializer syntax:

```
var stone1 = Go()
```

The preceding creates an instance of the Go structure, and the instance name is stone1. The property row and column are both initialized to 0 by default:

```
println(stone1.row)      //---0---
println(stone1.column)   //---0---
```

You access the properties using the dot (.) syntax. Just as you can access the value of the property, you can also change its value:

```
stone1.row = 12          //---change the row to 12---
stone1.column = 16       //---change the column to 16---
```

Memberwise Initializers

If the structure has a property that does not have a default value, you cannot use the default initializer syntax. In other words, if you don't initialize the value of row or column to some default value, the following statements will fail:

```
struct Go {
    var row:Int          //---no default value---
    var column:Int       //---no default value---
}

var stone1 = Go()        //---error---
```

To rectify this, you can use the *memberwise initializer* (which is automatically generated for you when you define a structure) to initialize the properties of a structure with certain values when it is created:

```
var stone1 = Go(row:12, column:16)
```

In the preceding example, when you create an instance of the Go structure, you also set the value for row and column.

Continuing with the Go example, a stone placed on the Go board is either black or white. Therefore, you can now define a new enumeration called StoneColor and add a color property to the Go structure:

```
enum StoneColor:String {
    case Black = "Black"
    case White = "White"
}

struct Go {
    var row:Int              //---0...18---
    var column:Int           //---0...18---
    var color:StoneColor
}
```

> **NOTE** *Enumeration is covered in more detail in Chapter 2.*

The color property is an enumeration of type StoneColor. To create an instance of the Go structure, use the memberwise initializer:

```
var stone1 = Go(row:12, column:16, color:StoneColor.Black)
```

Structures as Value Types

A structure is a value type. In other words, when you assign a variable/constant of a value type to another variable/constant, its value is copied over. Consider the following example:

```
var stone1 = Go(row:12, column:16, color:StoneColor.Black)
var stone2 = stone1

println("---Stone1---")
println(stone1.row)
println(stone1.column)
println(stone1.color.rawValue)
```

```
println("---Stone2---")
println(stone2.row)
println(stone2.column)
println(stone2.color.rawValue)
```

In the preceding code snippet, stone1 is assigned to stone2. Therefore, stone2 will now have the same value as stone1. This is evident by the values that are output by the preceding code snippet:

```
---Stone1---
12
16
Black
---Stone2---
12
16
Black
```

To prove that stone2's value is independent of stone1's, modify the value of stone1 as follows:

```
stone1.row = 6
stone1.column = 7
stone1.color = StoneColor.White
```

Then print out the values for both stones again:

```
println("===After modifications===")
println("---Stone1---")
println(stone1.row)
println(stone1.column)
println(stone1.color.rawValue)

println("---Stone2---")
println(stone2.row)
println(stone2.column)
println(stone2.color.rawValue)
```

The preceding statements print out the following, proving that the values of the two stones are independent of each other:

```
===After modifications===
---Stone1---
6
7
White
---Stone2---
12
16
Black
```

> **NOTE** In Swift, String, Array, and Dictionary types are implemented using structures. As such, when they are assigned to another variable, their values are always copied.

Comparing Structures

You cannot compare two structures using the == operator. This is because the compiler does not understand what defines two structures as being equal. Hence, you need to overload the default meaning of the == and != operators:

```
func == (stone1: Go, stone2: Go) -> Bool {
    return (stone1.row == stone2.row) &&
           (stone1.column == stone2.column) &&
           (stone1.color == stone2.color)
}

func != (stone1: Go, stone2: Go) -> Bool {
    return !(stone1 == stone2)
}
```

Essentially, the preceding two functions are overloading the two operators—equal (==) and not equal (!=). Each function takes two Go instances and returns a Bool value. Two instances are deemed to be the same if the row, column, and color properties of each instance are equal to the other instance.

You can now use the == operator to test whether stone1 and stone2 are of the same value:

```
var stone1 = Go(row:12, column:16, color:StoneColor.Black)
var stone2 = Go(row:12, column:16, color:StoneColor.Black)

if stone1 == stone2 {
    println("Same!")
} else {
    println("Different!")
}
```

The preceding code snippet will output the following:

```
Same!
```

CLASSES

A class is similar to a structure in many ways. Like a structure, a class defines properties to store values, contains initializers to initialize its properties' values, and so on. However, a class has additional capabilities not found in a structure. For example, you can use inheritance on a class to ensure that the class inherits the characteristics of another class, and you can also use de-initializers to free up resources when an instance of a class is destroyed. In this section, you will learn about the basics of a class and some of the features that are also applicable to structures.

> **NOTE** *Chapter 9 discusses class inheritance.*

Defining a Class

You define a class using the `class` keyword:

```
class ClassName {

}
```

Here is one example:

```
class MyPointClass {

}
```

The preceding code snippet defines a class called `MyPointClass`. When naming classes, the recommendation is to use UpperCamelCase (such as `MyPointClass`, `EmployeeInfo`, `CustomerDetails`, etc.). An important difference between Objective-C and Swift is that in Swift there is no need to have one file to declare a class and another file to define the implementation of a class; one file handles all the declaration and implementation.

To create an instance of a class, you call the class name followed by a pair of parentheses (`()`) and then assign it to a variable or constant:

```
var ptA = MyPointClass()
```

Properties

Like structures, classes also have properties. In Swift, there are two types of properties:

➤ **Stored property**—A constant or variable that is stored within an instance of a class or a structure. When you declare a variable or constant within a class or structure, that is a stored property.

➤ **Computed property**—These calculate values and typically return values. They can also optionally store values for other properties indirectly.

Stored Properties

You add stored properties to a class by declaring them just as you would normal variables and constants:

```
class MyPointClass {
    var x = 0.0      //---variable---
    var y = 0.0      //---variable---
    let width = 2    //---constant---
}
```

The preceding code snippet adds two variables to the `MyPointClass`—x, y (both `Double` properties), and a constant, `width` (`Int` property). In Swift, constants and variables that are stored within a class are known as *stored properties*. Like structures, stored properties can also have default values.

To access the stored properties of a class, you use dot notation (.) to access an individual property, as shown here:

```
var ptA = MyPointClass()

//---assigning values to properties---
ptA.x = 25.0
ptA.y = 50.0

//---retrieving values from properties---
println(ptA.x)          //---25.0---
println(ptA.y)          //---50.0---
println(ptA.width)      //---2---
```

> **NOTE** *Structures also support stored properties.*

PROPERTIES AND MEMBER VARIABLES

In other languages such as C# and Objective-C, properties are public-facing variables that users of the class can access. Internally within the class, member variables may be used to store the values of these properties. In Swift, this is not required. It provides a unified approach to properties—you just need to deal with the properties that you have declared in your class; no instance member variables are required to store the values.

Lazy Stored Properties

Sometimes a class itself may contain a property that references another class. Consider the following example:

```
class PointMath {
    //---contains methods to calculate distances related to the point---
    var someValue = 1.2345
}

class MyPointClass {
    var x = 0.0
    var y = 0.0
    let width = 2
    var pointMath = PointMath()
}
```

Here, the MyPointClass class contains a property of type PointMath. By default, when you create an instance of MyPointClass, the PointMath class would also be instantiated. If the PointMath class contains methods that take a long time to instantiate, it would hence be computationally expensive every time you try to create a MyPointClass object.

You can use the `lazy` keyword to mark a property as a *lazy stored property*:

```
class MyPointClass {
    var x = 0.0
    var y = 0.0
    let width = 2
    lazy var pointMath = PointMath()
}
```

When the `pointMath` property is marked as a lazy stored property, it will not be instantiated when the `MyPointClass` is instantiated. Instead, it will only be instantiated when you access the `pointMath` property:

```
println(ptA.pointMath.someValue) //---1.2345---
```

> **NOTE** *Lazy stored properties must always be declared as a variable using the* var *keyword (and not as a constant using the* let *keyword). This is because a lazy stored property's value is not known until it is first accessed.*

Computed Properties

Whereas stored properties store actual values, *computed properties* do not. Computed properties enable you to set or retrieve another property's value. The best way to understand this is with an example.

Using the same `MyPointClass` class, you now have the additional computed property called `newPosition`:

```
class MyPointClass {
    var x = 0.0
    var y = 0.0
    let width = 2
    lazy var pointMath = PointMath()

    var newPosition:(Double, Double) {
        get {
            return (x, y)
        }
        set (position) {      //---position is a tuple---
            x = position.0  //---x---
            y = position.1  //---y---
        }
    }
}
```

The `newPosition` property is a *computed property*. It accepts and returns a tuple containing two `Double` values. To use the `newPosition` property, you can assign it a tuple:

```
var ptB = MyPointClass()

//---assign a tuple to the newPosition property---
ptB.newPosition = (10.0,15.0)
```

```
println(ptB.x) //---10.0---
println(ptB.y) //---15.0---
```

When you assign it a value, the set (known as the *setter*) block of the code is executed:

```
set (position) {     //---position is a tuple---
    x = position.0
    y = position.1
}
```

Here, the position represents the tuple that you have just assigned ((10.0,15.0))—position.0 represents the first value in the tuple (10.0) and position.1 represents the second value in the tuple (15.0). You assign these values to the x and y properties, respectively.

When you try to access the newPosition property, as shown here:

```
var position = ptB.newPosition
println(position.0)   //---10.0---
println(position.1)   //---15.0---
```

it will execute the get (known as the *getter*) block of code:

```
get {
    return (x, y)
}
```

In this case, it returns the value of x and y using a tuple. Because the newPosition property does not store any value itself, but rather stores the value assigned to it in another property, it is known as a computed property.

> **NOTE** Structures also support computed properties.

Motivation Behind Computed Properties

At first glance, the computed property feature in Swift doesn't look very useful. After all, you could use stored properties for most cases. To understand the usefulness of computed properties, consider another example:

```
class Distance {
    var miles = 0.0
    var km: Double {
        get {
            return 1.60934 * miles
        }
        set (km) {
            miles = km / 1.60934
        }
    }
}
```

In the preceding code snippet, you have the `Distance` class—it has a stored property named `miles`, which enables you to store the distance in miles. You also have a `km` computed property. The `km` computed property enables you to retrieve the distance in kilometers:

```
var d = Distance()
d.miles  = 10.0
println(d.km)       //---16.0934---
```

It also enables you to store a distance in kilometers:

```
d.km = 20.0
println(d.miles)   //---12.4274547329961---
```

Observe that in this case, the actual distance is stored in miles, not kilometers. That way, you only need to store the distance once, and not worry about having additional stored properties to store the distance in other units. If you needed to return the distance in yards, you would just need to add the computed property as shown here:

```
class Distance {
    var miles = 0.0
    var km: Double {
        get {
            return 1.60934 * miles
        }
        set (km) {
            miles = km / 1.60934
        }
    }
    var yard:Double {
        get{
            return miles * 1760
        }
        set (yard) {
            miles = yard / 1760
        }
    }
}
```

The following code snippet shows how you could use the newly added computed property:

```
d.miles = 1.0
println(d.yard)    //---1760.0---

d.yard = 234567
println(d.miles)   //---133.276704545455---
```

The newValue keyword

Earlier you used the name `position` to define the tuple that contains the new position:

```
var newPosition:(Double, Double) {
    get {
        return (x, y)
    }
    set (position) {     //---position is a tuple---
```

```
            x = position.0  //---x---
            y = position.1  //---y---
        }
    }
```

If you did not define a name for the tuple, you can use the shorthand name of newValue, as shown here:

```
    var newPosition:(Double, Double) {
        get {
            return (x, y)
        }
        set {  //---newValue (shorthand name) is a tuple---
            x = newValue.0
            y = newValue.1
        }
    }
```

Read-Only Computed Properties

A computed property with a getter but no setter is known as a *read-only computed property*. A read-only computed property can be accessed but not set. The following shows the newPosition computed property without the setter:

```
    var newPosition:(Double, Double) {
        get {
            return (x, y)
        }
    }
```

A read-only computed property can also be simplified without the use of the get keyword:

```
    var newPosition:(Double, Double) {
        return (x, y)
    }
```

In either case, you can no longer set a value to the newPosition property:

```
    var ptB = MyPointClass()
    ptB.x = 25.0
    ptB.y = 50.0

    //---assign a tuple to the newPosition property---
    ptB.newPosition = (10,15)  //---error---
```

> **NOTE** *If a computed property has a setter, it must also have a getter.*

Property Observers

Recall earlier in the discussion about stored properties the example of the MyPointClass, with three stored properties:

```
    class MyPointClass {
        var x = 0.0
```

```
    var y = 0.0
    let width = 2
```

You can access the properties by specifying the property name using the dot syntax:

```
var ptA = MyPointClass()
//---assigning values to properties---
ptA.x = 15.0
ptA.y = 50.0
```

However, what if you need to enforce a range of valid numbers for both x and y? For example, suppose the maximum allowable value for x is 100 and the minimum is –100. In this case, you can use *property observers* to observe and respond to changes in the properties' values.

In Swift, you can use two property observers:

➤   willSet—Fired before a property value is stored

➤   didSet—Fired immediately after a value is stored

To see how these property observers work, take a look at the following code snippet:

```
class MyPointClass {
    var x: Double = 0.0 {
        willSet(newX) {
            println("Going to assign a value of \(newX) to x")
        }
        didSet {
            println("Value of x before assignment : \(oldValue)")
            println("Value of x after assignment : \(x)")
            if x>100 || x<(-100) {
                x = oldValue
            }
        }
    }
}
```

In the preceding code snippet, the willSet block of code will be executed when you try to assign a value to the x property. It will be fired before the value is assigned to x. After the value is assigned, the didSet block of code will execute. In this example, if the assigned value is less than -100 or greater than 100, then the old value of the property is restored.

If you do not specify a name after the willSet keyword, you can still retrieve the new value using the newValue keyword. Similarly, you can also specify a name after the didSet keyword; if not, the old value of the property can be retrieved using the oldValue keyword.

> **NOTE** *Property observers apply only to stored properties. For computed properties, you can use a setter to check the validity of a value before assigning it to a property.*

> **NOTE** *Property observers are not called when a property is first initialized. They will only be called when a property is modified outside of initialization.*

Typed Properties

All the properties you have seen until this point are *instance properties*. Instance properties belong to an instance of a particular type. In contrast, *type properties* pertain to a class.

> **NOTE** *Typed properties are commonly known as static properties or class properties in other programming languages such as Java, C#, and Objective-C.*

Unlike instance properties, typed properties are accessed using the class name. Consider the following example:

```
class MyPointClass {
    var x = 0.0
    var y = 0.0
    let width = 2
    lazy var pointMath = PointMath()

    class var origin:(Double, Double) {
        get {
            return (0,0)
        }
    }

    var newPosition:(Double, Double) {
        get {
            return (x, y)
        }
        set (position) {      //---position is a tuple---
            x = position.0  //---x---
            y = position.1  //---y---
        }
    }
}
```

> **NOTE** *For classes, only computed type properties are supported. For structures, both stored and computed type properties are supported. For structures, you use the* static *keyword instead of the* class *keyword to denote a typed property.*

In the preceding example, `origin` is a typed property—it is prefixed with the `class` keyword. To access the typed property, use its class name and call it directly:

```
println(MyPointClass.origin)     //---(0.0, 0.0)---
```

Typed properties are useful for cases in which a property needs to have the same value across instances.

Initializers

When you create an instance of a class using a pair of empty parentheses, you are calling its *default initializer*:

```
var ptA = MyPointClass()
```

> **NOTE** The compiler can only generate the default initializer if all the properties within the class have default values.

The compiler automatically generates the default initializer; there is no need for you to define it. Sometimes, however, you do want to initialize certain properties to specific values when an instance of the class is created. To do that, you can define an initializer using the special name `init`:

```
class MyPointClass {
    var x = 0.0
    var y = 0.0
    let width = 2
    lazy var pointMath = PointMath()

    init() {
        x = 5.0
        y = 5.0
    }
}
```

> **NOTE** Unlike Objective-C, initializers in Swift do not return a value.

The `init()` initializer is automatically called when you create an instance of a class using a pair of empty parentheses:

```
var ptB = MyPointClass()
println(ptB.x)              //---5.0---
println(ptB.y)              //---5.0---
println(ptB.width)          //---2---
```

When you create an instance of the `MyPointClass`, the value of both `x` and `y` is set to 5, as is evident in the output.

You can also create parameterized initializers by allowing the user of the class to pass in arguments through the initializers. The following example shows another initializer with two parameters:

```
class MyPointClass {
    var x = 0.0
    var y = 0.0
    let width = 2
    lazy var pointMath = PointMath()

    init() {
        x = 5.0
        y = 5.0
    }

    init(x:Double, y:Double) {
        self.x = x
        self.y = y
    }
}
```

When you create an instance of the class, you can call the initializer by passing it two arguments:

```
var ptC = MyPointClass(x:7.0, y:8.0)
println(ptC.x)          //---7.0---
println(ptC.y)          //---8.0---
println(ptC.width)      //---2---
```

Initializers and External Parameter Names

Note that you need to specify the external parameter names for the initializer with two parameters:

```
var ptC = MyPointClass(x:7.0, y:8.0)
```

Unlike function names, an initializer does not have a name (it is simply identified by the special name init); thus, the following initializers are valid:

```
class MyPointClass {
    var x = 0.0
    var y = 0.0
    let width = 2
    lazy var pointMath = PointMath()

    init() {
        x = 5.0
        y = 5.0
    }

    init(x:Double, y:Double) {
        self.x = x
        self.y = y
    }

    init(y:Double, x:Double) {
```

```
            self.x = x
            self.y = y
        }
    }
```

The only way to differentiate between the second and third initializers is to specify the external parameter names when calling them. If you want to omit the external parameter name, you can do so by prefixing the parameter name with an underscore (_), as shown here:

```
class MyPointClass {
    var x = 0.0
    var y = 0.0
    let width = 2
    lazy var pointMath = PointMath()

    init() {
        x = 5.0
        y = 5.0
    }

    init(_ x:Double, _ y:Double) {
        self.x = x
        self.y = y
    }

    init(y:Double, x:Double) {
        self.x = x
        self.y = y
    }
}
```

In this case, you can call the second initializer without specifying the external parameter names:

```
var ptC = MyPointClass(7.0, 8.0)
```

Once the external parameter names are omitted, you can no longer call the second initializer with their external parameter names:

```
var ptC = MyPointClass(x:7.0, y:8.0)   //---not allowed---
```

You can continue to call the third initializer using the external parameter names:

```
var ptC = MyPointClass(y:8.0, x:7.0)
```

Of course, if you were to prefix the parameter names in the third initializer with underscores, you would run into a problem:

```
    init(_ x:Double, _ y:Double) {
        self.x = x
        self.y = y
    }

    init(_ y:Double, _ x:Double) {
```

```
        self.x = x
        self.y = y
    }
```

In this case, the compiler will generate an error message because it sees two initializers with the same parameter type (see Figure 8-2).

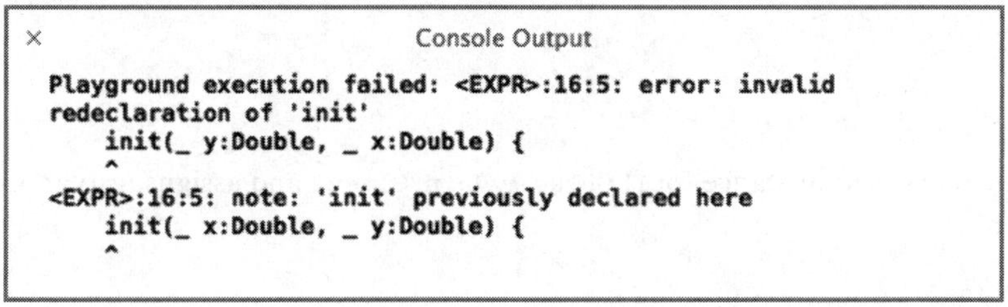

```
×                    Console Output

 Playground execution failed: <EXPR>:16:5: error: invalid
 redeclaration of 'init'
     init(_ y:Double, _ x:Double) {
     ^
 <EXPR>:16:5: note: 'init' previously declared here
     init(_ x:Double, _ y:Double) {
     ^
```

FIGURE 8-2

Initializing Variables and Constants During Initialization

As mentioned earlier, the compiler automatically generates a default initializer if the properties are initialized to their default values. Suppose you have the following class definition:

```
class MyPointClass2 {
    var x: Double
    var y: Double
    let width: Int
}
```

The preceding class definition will not compile, as the compiler cannot find the default values for the properties. However, if you were to add an initializer that initializes the properties' values, this would compile:

```
class MyPointClass2 {
    var x: Double
    var y: Double
    let width: Int

    init() {
        x = 0.0
        y = 0.0
        width = 2
    }
}
```

Classes as Reference Types

Unlike structures, classes are reference types. This means that when an instance of a class is assigned to another variable or constant, a reference is made to the original instance instead of creating a new copy. To see what this means, assume you have the following `MyPointClass2` class:

```
class MyPointClass2 {
    var x: Double
    var y: Double
    let width: Int

    init() {
        x = 0.0
        y = 0.0
        width = 2
    }
}
```

The following code snippet creates an instance (pt1) of the MyPointClass2 and assigns it to another variable pt2:

```
var pt1 = MyPointClass2()
pt1.x = 25.0
pt1.y = 50.0
var pt2 = pt1
```

Figure 8-3 shows what happens when pt1 is assigned to pt2.

Both variables are pointing to the same instance of MyPointClass2. When you print out the properties of each instance:

```
println("---pt1---")
println(pt1.x)
println(pt1.y)

println("---pt2---")
println(pt1.x)
println(pt1.y)
```

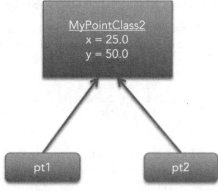

FIGURE 8-3

you will get the following:

```
---pt1---
25.0
50.0
---pt2---
25.0
50.0
```

Make some changes to pt1 and print out the properties of both variables again:

```
pt1.x = 35
pt1.y = 76

println("===After modifications===")
println("---pt1---")
println(pt1.x)
println(pt1.y)

println("---pt2---")
```

```
println(pt1.x)
println(pt1.y)
```

You will now see that the values for both instances' properties have changed, proving that both variables are indeed pointing to the same instance:

```
===After modifications===
---pt1---
35.0
76.0
---pt2---
35.0
76.0
```

Comparing Instances—Identity Operators

Often, you need to compare two instances of a class to determine if they are the same. There are two types of comparison that you will perform:

➤ Compare whether two variables are pointing to the same instance.

➤ Compare whether two instances have the same value.

To illustrate the first, consider the following example. Suppose you have the following three instances of MyPointClass2—pt1, pt2, and pt3:

```
var pt1 = MyPointClass2()
pt1.x = 25.0
pt1.y = 50.0

var pt2 = pt1

var pt3 = MyPointClass2()
pt3.x = 25.0
pt3.y = 50.0
```

Figure 8-4 shows that pt1 and pt2 are both pointing to the same instance, while pt3 is pointing to another instance.

To check whether pt1 and pt2 are pointing to the same instance, use the *identical to* (===) operator:

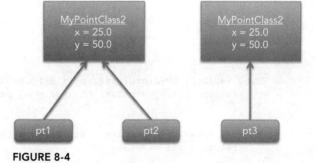

FIGURE 8-4

```
if pt1 === pt2 {
    println("pt1 is identical to pt2")
} else {
    println("pt1 is not identical to pt2")
}
```

The preceding code snippet will output the following:

```
pt1 is identical to pt2
```

The next code snippet checks whether `pt1` and `pt3` are pointing to the same instance:

```
if pt1 === pt3 {
    println("pt1 is identical to pt3")
} else {
    println("pt1 is not identical to pt3")
}
```

The preceding code snippet will output the following:

```
pt1 is not identical to pt3
```

Besides the identical to (===) operator, Swift also supports the not identical to (!==) operator.

Comparing Instances—Equivalence Operators

In the previous section, you used the identity operator to determine whether two variables are pointing to the same instances of a class. However, a lot of times you will also be interested to know if two instances are actually the "same"—i.e., if they have the same values. In Swift, the compiler doesn't know what qualifies as the "same" values for your custom types; hence, you need to define that meaning yourself through operator overloading.

The following code snippet includes the definition of the `MyPointClass2` class, as well as two operator overloading functions:

```
class MyPointClass2 {
    var x: Double
    var y: Double
    let width: Int

    init() {
        x = 0.0
        y = 0.0
        width = 2
    }
}

func == (ptA: MyPointClass2, ptB: MyPointClass2) -> Bool {
    return (ptA.x == ptB.x) && (ptA.y == ptB.y)
}

func != (ptA: MyPointClass2, ptB: MyPointClass2) -> Bool {
    return !(ptA == ptB)
}
```

Essentially, the two functions are overloading the two operators: equal (==) and not equal (!=). Each function takes two `MyPointClass2` instances and returns a `Bool` value. Two instances are deemed to be the same if the x and y properties of each instance are equal to the other instance.

You can now use the == operator to test if `pt1` and `pt3` have the same value:

```
var pt1 = MyPointClass2()
pt1.x = 25.0
```

```
pt1.y = 50.0
var pt2 = pt1

var pt3 = MyPointClass2()
pt3.x = 25.0
pt3.y = 50.0

if pt1 == pt3 {
    println("pt1 is same as pt3")
} else {
    println("pt1 is not the same as pt3")
}
```

The preceding will output the following:

```
pt1 is same as pt3
```

You can also use the != operator to compare the two instances:

```
if pt1 != pt3 {
    println("pt1 is not the same as pt3")
} else {
    println("pt1 is same as pt3")
}
```

Methods in Classes

In Swift, you define methods just like how you define functions. There are two types of methods in Swift:

➤ **Instance methods**—Belong to a particular instance of a class

➤ **Type methods**—Belong to the class

Instance Methods

An instance method is a function that belongs to a particular instance of a class. The following Car class has four instance methods—accelerate(), decelerate(), stop(), and printSpeed():

```
class Car {
    var speed = 0

    func accelerate() {
        speed += 10
        if speed > 80 {
            speed = 80
        }
        printSpeed()
    }

    func decelerate() {
        speed -= 10
        if speed<0 {
```

```
            speed = 0
        }
        printSpeed()
    }

    func stop() {
        while speed>0 {
            decelerate()
        }
    }

    func printSpeed() {
        println("Speed: \(speed)")
    }
}
```

To call the methods, you need to first create an instance of the Car class:

```
var c = Car()
```

Once the instance has been created, you can call the methods using dot notation (.):

```
c.accelerate()    //---10---
c.accelerate()    //---20---
c.accelerate()    //---30---
c.accelerate()    //---40---
c.decelerate()    //---30---
c.stop()          //---20---
                  //---10---
                  //---0---
```

Local and External Parameter Names for Methods

The four methods in the Car class have no parameters. Therefore, let's add two more methods to the Car class:

```
class Car {
    var speed = 0
    func accelerate() {
        speed += 10
        if speed > 80 {
            speed = 80
        }
        printSpeed()
    }

    func accelerateBy(quantum: Int) {
        speed += quantum
        if speed > 80 {
            speed = 80
        }
        printSpeed()
    }

    func accelerateBy(quantum: Int, repeat:Int) {
```

```
        for index in 1...repeat {
            speed += quantum
            if speed >= 80 {
                speed = 80
                break
            }
            printSpeed()
        }
        printSpeed()
    }

    func decelerate() {
        speed -= 10
        if speed<0 {
            speed = 0
        }
        printSpeed()
    }

    func stop() {
        while speed>0 {
            decelerate()
        }
    }

    func printSpeed() {
        println("Speed: \(speed)")
    }
}
```

In this case you have two additional methods:

➤   accelerateBy()—Takes an Int argument

➤   accelerateBy()—Takes two Int arguments

To call the first method, you need to pass in an integer argument:

```
c.accelerateBy(5)
```

To call the second method, you need to pass in an integer value for the first and second arguments, and in addition you need to specify the external parameter name for the *second* argument:

```
c.accelerateBy(5, repeat:10)
```

> **NOTE** *In Swift, the first parameter in a method is a local parameter name by default, while subsequent parameters are both local and external parameter names.*

If you want to make the first parameter an external parameter name, prefix it with the hash (#) tag, as shown here:

```
func accelerateBy(# quantum: Int, repeat:Int) {
```

```
    ...
}
```

You now need to specify the external parameter name for the first argument:

```
c.accelerateBy(quantum:5, repeat:10)
```

If you do not wish the second or subsequent parameter names to be exposed as external parameter names, prefix the parameter name with an underscore (_):

```
func accelerateBy(quantum: Int, _ repeat:Int) {
    ...
}
```

You now don't have to specify the external parameter name for the second argument:

```
c.accelerateBy(5, 10)
```

The self Property

Every instance of a class has an implicit property known as self. The self property refers to the instance of the class, hence its name. Recall from earlier the property named speed:

```
class Car {
    var speed = 0

    func accelerate() {
        speed += 10
        if speed > 80 {
            speed = 80
        }
        printSpeed()
    }
    ...
```

Because speed is declared within the class, you can also rewrite the preceding by prefixing speed with self:

```
class Car {
    var speed = 0

    func accelerate() {
        self.speed += 10
        if self.speed > 80 {
            self.speed = 80
        }
        printSpeed()
    }

    ...
```

In most cases, prefixing a property using the self keyword is redundant. However, there are cases for which this is actually useful and mandatory. Consider the following example:

```
class Car {
   var speed = 0

   func setInitialSpeed(speed: Int) {
      self.speed = speed
   }

   ...
```

In this example, the parameter name for the setInitialSpeed() method is also named speed, which is the same as the property named speed. To differentiate between the two, you use the self keyword to identify the property.

Type Methods

As opposed to instance methods, type methods are methods that belong to the class. Type methods are called directly using the class name, not through instances of the class.

> **NOTE** *In Swift, structures, classes, and enumerations support type methods.*

Type methods are declared similarly to instance methods, except that they are prefixed with the class keyword. The following code snippet shows that the Car class has the class method named kilometersToMiles():

```
class Car {
   var speed = 0
   class func kilometersToMiles(km:Int) -> Double{
      return Double(km) / 1.60934
   }

   ...
```

To use the kilometersToMiles() method, use the class name and call the method directly:

```
c.speed = 30
var s = Car.kilometersToMiles(c.speed)
println("\(s) mph")    //---18.6411820994942 mph---
```

Class methods are often used for utility functions, where implementation is independent of each instance of the class.

Methods in Structures

Methods are not exclusive to classes. Structures can also have methods. Consider the earlier example of the Go structure:

```
enum StoneColor:String {
   case Black = "Black"
   case White = "White"
```

```
    }
struct Go {
    var row:Int
    var column:Int
    var color:StoneColor
}
```

You could add a `printPosition()` method to output the position of a stone on the Go board:

```
struct Go {
    var row:Int
    var column:Int
    var color:StoneColor

    func printPosition() {
        println("[" + String(row) + "," + String(column) + "]")
    }
}
```

To use the `printPosition()` method, simply create an instance of the `Go` structure and call the `printPosition()` method directly:

```
var stone1 = Go(row:12, column:16, color:StoneColor.Black)
stone1.printPosition()   //---[12,16]---
```

Consider another method named `move()`, which moves the stone according to the specified rows and columns:

```
struct Go {
    var row:Int             //---0...18---
    var column:Int          //---0...18---
    var color:StoneColor

    func printPosition() {
        println("[" + String(row) + "," + String(column) + "]")
    }

    func move(dRow: Int, dColumn: Int) {
        row += dRow
        column += dColumn
    }
}
```

However, the preceding method will not compile. In Swift, the properties of a value type cannot be modified from within its instance method; and because a structure is a value type, and the preceding `move()` method is trying to modify the `row` and `column` properties, the preceding will fail. To fix this, you need to explicitly indicate that the method is *mutating*, as shown here:

```
struct Go {
    var row:Int             //---0...18---
    var column:Int          //---0...18---
    var color:StoneColor

    func printPosition() {
        println("[" + String(row) + "," + String(column) + "]")
```

```
    }

    mutating func move(dRow: Int, dColumn: Int) {
        row += dRow
        column += dColumn
    }
}
```

You can now move the stone by calling the `move()` method:

```
var stone1 = Go(row:12, column:16, color:StoneColor.Black)
stone1.printPosition()
stone1.move(2, dColumn: 1)
stone1.printPosition()    //---[14,17]---
```

What actually happens behind the scenes is that the `move()` method makes changes to the original structure (`stone1` in this example), returns a new instance of the structure, and then overwrites the original instance. Because of this, the `stone1` structure must be declared as a variable using the `var` keyword. If `stone1` is a constant (declared using the `let` keyword), the `move()` method will cause an error:

```
let stone1 = Go(row:12, column:16, color:StoneColor.Black)
stone1.printPosition()
stone1.move(2, dColumn: 1)    //---error---
```

This is because the `move()` method is attempting to modify an immutable structure.

SUMMARY

In this chapter, you have seen how structures and classes are defined. You have also seen how a structure or class can have the following:

➤ Methods

➤ Properties

➤ Initializers

One important feature of Swift is the various types of properties available, which differs from conventional OOP languages. In Swift, structures behave very much like classes, with a notable exception: Structures are value types and classes are reference types. In the next chapter, you will learn another important topic in Swift OOP: inheritance.

EXERCISES

1. Create a structure named DOB to store a date containing the year, month, and day.

2. Create a structure to store the information of a student. The structure needs to be able to store the following information:

   a. Student ID (String)

   b. Student Name (String)

   c. Date of birth (DOB [from question #1])

3. Add a computed property named age to the structure defined in question #2 so that you can obtain the age of a student.

4. Create an instance of the structure that you have created in question #3.

5. Print out the age of the student.

▶ WHAT YOU LEARNED IN THIS CHAPTER

TOPIC	KEY CONCEPTS
Structures	A structure is a special kind of data type that groups a list of variables and places them under a unified name.
Memberwise initializer	Use the memberwise initializer to initialize the values of a structure's members.
Structures as a value type	A structure is a value type—i.e., when you assign a variable/constant of a value type to another variable/constant, its value is copied over.
Comparing structures	You need to overload the == and != operators.
Classes	A class is similar to a structure in many ways. Like a structure, a class defines properties to store values, contains initializers to initialize its properties' values, and so on.
Properties	Two types of properties are supported: stored and computed.
Stored properties	A stored property directly stores the value of a property within a class.
Computed properties	A computed property does not directly store the value of a property within a class; it stores it using another property.
Storing values in computed properties	You use the get{} and set{} to store values in computed properties.
Lazy stored properties	A property that is marked as lazy will not be instantiated until it is actually used.
Property observers	Property observers let you handle events that are fired before and after the value of a stored property is assigned.
Typed properties	Typed property is a property belonging to a class, not an instance.
Initializers	When you create an instance of a class using a pair of empty parentheses, you are calling its default initializer. You can also create your own initializer using the special init() function name.
Initializers and external parameter names	By default, you need to explicitly specify the parameter names when calling an initializer.
Classes as reference types	Classes are reference types. This means that when an instance of a class is assigned to another variable or constant, a reference is made to the original instance instead of creating a new copy.

continues

(continued)

TOPIC	KEY CONCEPTS
Comparing class instances	Use the identical to (===) and not identical (!==) operators.
Comparing class equivalence	You need to overload the == and != operators.
Methods in classes	Two types of methods—instance and type methods.
Local and external parameter names for methods	In Swift, the first parameter in a method is a local parameter name by default, whereas subsequent parameters are both local and external parameter names.
Methods in structures	In Swift, the properties of a value type cannot be modified from within its instance method; to do so requires the `mutating` keyword.

Inheritance

WHAT YOU WILL LEARN IN THIS CHAPTER:

➤ What inheritance is

➤ How to define and instantiate a base class

➤ How to create an abstract class

➤ How to inherit a base class

➤ How to override methods

➤ How to override initializers

➤ How to overload initializers

➤ How to create abstract methods

➤ How to overload methods

➤ How to prevent subclassing

➤ The different types of initializers

➤ How to perform initializer chaining

➤ How to call initializers in subclasses

➤ Using extensions in Swift

➤ Using access controls in Swift

In the previous chapter, you learned how classes are defined and how to add methods and properties to a class. In this chapter, you continue to explore object-oriented programming (OOP) by looking at another important topic—inheritance. In addition, you will also learn about access controls and how Swift's interpretation of access control is different from conventional programming languages.

UNDERSTANDING INHERITANCE

Class inheritance is one of the cornerstones of OOP. It basically means that a class can inherit the properties and methods from another class. Class inheritance enables a high degree of code reuse, allowing the same implementation to be adapted for another use. Swift fully supports the capability of class inheritance.

> **NOTE** *This chapter assumes that you already have a good understanding of OOP. Readers who would like more detailed information about object-oriented programming concepts should check out* Code Complete: A Practical Handbook of Software Construction, Second Edition, *by Steve McConnell (Microsoft Press).*

Defining a Base Class

A *base class* is simply a class that does not inherit from another class. For example, the following Shape class does not inherit from any class, and hence it is known as a base class:

```
class Shape {
    //---stored properties---
    var length:Double = 0
    var width:Double = 0

    func perimeter() -> Double {
        return 2 * (length + width)
    }
}
```

The Shape class contains two stored properties, length and width, as well as a perimeter() method. This class does not assume that an object has any particular shape; it also assumes that an object has a measurable length and width, and that its perimeter is twice the sum of its length and width.

Instantiating a Base Class

As you have learned in the previous chapter, you can create an instance of this class using the default initializer:

```
var shape = Shape()
```

However, it is really not very meaningful to create an instance of the Shape class, as it does not tell you much about the exact shape that you are dealing with. In real life, an object may have various shapes—such as, but not limited to, the following:

➤ Rectangle

➤ Circle

➤ Square

➤ Rhombus

Thus, it would be better to create classes that inherit the Shape base class, and extend from it if necessary.

Creating an Abstract Class

OOP includes the concept of abstract classes. Abstract classes are classes from which you cannot directly instantiate. In other words, you cannot create an instance of the class directly. Rather, you can only create an instance of its subclass. In Swift, abstract classes are not supported, so you should use protocols to implement the concept of abstract classes if you need to do so.

> **NOTE** *Chapter 11 discusses the concept of protocols in more details.*

However, you can improvise an abstract method by using the private identifier together with an initializer, as shown here:

```
class Shape {
    //---stored properties---
    var length:Double = 0
    var width:Double = 0

    //---improvision to make the class abstract---
    private init() {
        length = 0
        width = 0
    }

    func perimeter() -> Double {
        return 2 * (length + width)
    }
}
```

In the preceding code snippet, you added a private initializer, init(), which limits its accessibility to within its physical file. That is to say, any code that is outside the physical file in which the Shape class is defined (say, Shape.swift) will not be able to call the initializer method. Therefore, when you create an instance of the Shape class, you will get an error (see Figure 9-1).

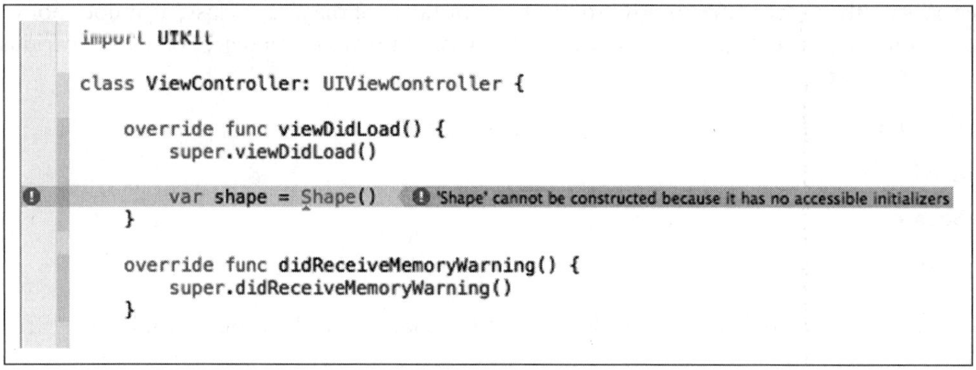

```
import UIKit

class ViewController: UIViewController {

    override func viewDidLoad() {
        super.viewDidLoad()

        var shape = Shape()    ! 'Shape' cannot be constructed because it has no accessible initializers
    }

    override func didReceiveMemoryWarning() {
        super.didReceiveMemoryWarning()
    }
}
```

FIGURE 9-1

> **NOTE** *You will learn more about the access controls mechanism in Swift later in this chapter.*

Inheriting from a Base Class

To inherit from a base class, you create another class and specify the base class name after the colon (:):

```
class Rectangle: Shape {

}
```

In the preceding code snippet, Rectangle is a subclass of Shape. That means it will inherit all the properties and methods declared in the Shape class. However, you are still not able to create an instance of the Rectangle class yet, because you need to create an initializer for the Rectangle class.

Overriding Initializers

As discussed earlier, the Shape class has a private initializer that is only visible to code that resides in the same physical file as the Shape class. In order to be able to create an instance of the Rectangle class, you need to provide an initializer, as shown here:

```
class Rectangle: Shape {
    //---override the init() initializer---
    override init() {
        super.init()
    }
}
```

Observe that you need to prefix the init() initializer with the override keyword. This is because the init() initializer is already in the base class (Shape). In addition, because you are overriding the initializer, you need to call the immediate superclass's `init()` method before exiting this initializer:

```
override init() {
    super.init()
}
```

You will now be able to create an instance of the `Rectangle` class:

```
var rectangle = Rectangle()
```

You can also access the `length` and `width` properties of the `Shape` base class:

```
rectangle.length = 5
rectangle.width = 6
```

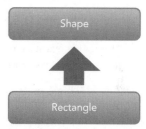

The following example shows how you can also access the `perimeter()` method defined in the `Shape` class:

```
println(rectangle.perimeter()) //---22.0---
```

Figure 9-2 shows the class hierarchy diagram of the `Rectangle` class.

FIGURE 9-2

Overloading Initializers

In the previous section, you override the default `init()` initializer. You can also add another initializer to the `Rectangle` class:

```
class Rectangle: Shape {
    //---override the init() initializer---
    override init() {
        super.init()
    }

    //---overload the init() initializer---
    init(length:Double, width:Double) {
        super.init()
        self.length = length
        self.width = width
    }
}
```

In this case, you are *overloading* the initializer with two parameters: `length` and `width`.

You can now create an instance of the `Rectangle` class like this:

```
var rectangle = Rectangle(length: 5,width: 6)
```

In Xcode, code completion will automatically display two initializers that you can use for the `Rectangle` class (see Figure 9-3).

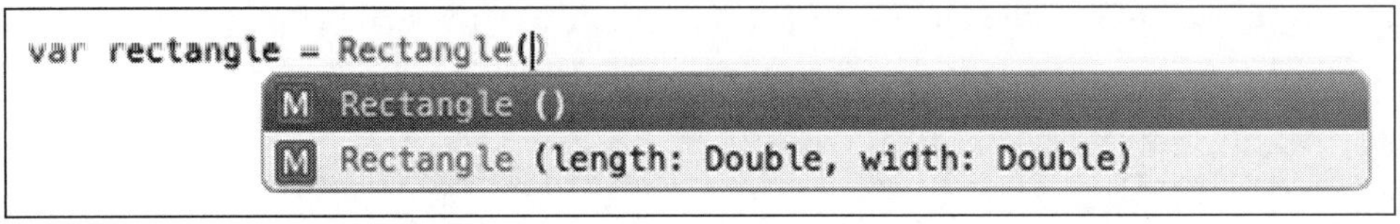

```
var rectangle = Rectangle(|)
            M  Rectangle ()
            M  Rectangle (length: Double, width: Double)
```

FIGURE 9-3

Swift adopts the following rules for initializers:

➤ If a subclass does not have any initializers, then all the base class' initializers are available to the subclass.

➤ If a subclass has at least one initializer, then it will hide all the initializers in the base class.

Here is an example to illustrate the preceding rules. The following `Square` class inherits from the `Rectangle` class (which has two overloaded initializers):

```
class Square: Rectangle {

}
```

When creating an instance of the `Square` class, you would see two initializers (see Figure 9-4).

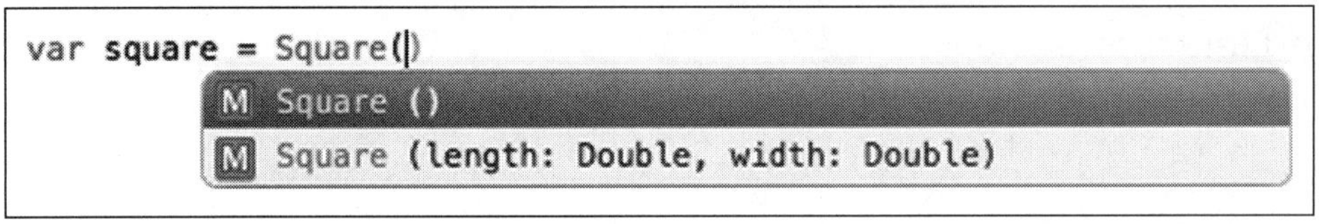

```
var square = Square(|)
            M  Square ()
            M  Square (length: Double, width: Double)
```

FIGURE 9-4

However, suppose the `Square` class has its own initializer, as shown here:

```
class Square: Rectangle {
    //---initializer---
    init(length:Double) {
        super.init()
        self.length = length
        self.width = self.length
    }
}
```

You will now be able to call only this initializer (see Figure 9-5). All the initializers in the base class (`Rectangle`) will be hidden.

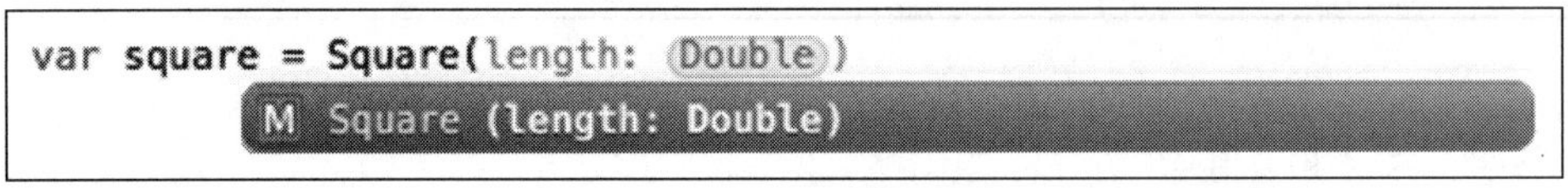

```
var square = Square(length: Double )
            M  Square (length: Double)
```

FIGURE 9-5

Creating Abstract Methods

As you likely know, OOP also includes the concept of abstract methods. An abstract method is a method that is declared in the base class but whose implementation is left to the inheriting class. Using the same Shape example, suppose you have an area() method in the Shape class, as shown here:

```
class Shape {
    //---stored properties---
    var length:Double = 0
    var width:Double = 0

    //---improvision to make the class abstract---
    private init() {
        length = 0
        width = 0
    }

    func perimeter() -> Double {
        return 2 * (length + width)
    }

    //---calculate the area of a shape---
    func area() -> Double {}
}
```

Ideally, the implementation of area() should be left to inheriting classes, as only specific shapes know how to calculate the area.

However, you cannot leave the implementation of the area() method empty, as shown in the preceding example. Swift does not support the concept of abstract methods. Rather, you should implement this using protocols.

There is, however, a way to improvise abstract methods—by using the assert() function:

```
class Shape {
    //---stored properties---
    var length:Double = 0
    var width:Double = 0

    //---improvision to make the class abstract---
    private init() {
        length = 0
        width = 0
    }

    func perimeter() -> Double {
        return 2 * (length + width)
    }

    //---improvision to make the method abstract---
    func area() -> Double {
        assert(false, "This method must be overridden")
    }
}
```

The `assert()` function takes two arguments: a condition and a message. When the condition evaluates to `false`, the program stops execution and the message is displayed.

> **NOTE** A good way to understand the `assert()` function is to think of its equivalent meaning in English—ensure. In other words, the assert statement means something like "ensure that the condition is true; otherwise, stop the program and display the message."

In fact, if you call the `area()` method through the `rectangle` instance, as shown in the following example, the code will crash, as indicated in Figure 9-6:

```
var rectangle = Rectangle(length: 5,width: 6)
println(rectangle.area())
```

```
class Shape {
    //----stored properties---
    var length:Double = 0
    var width:Double = 0

    //---improvision to make the class abstract---
    private init() {
        length = 0
        width = 0
    }

    func perimeter() -> Double {
        return 2 * (length + width)
    }

    //---improvision to make the method abstract---
    func area() -> Double {
        assert(false, "This method must be overridden")
    }                   Thread 1: EXC_BAD_INSTRUCTION (code=EXC_I386_INVOP, subcode=0x0)
}
```

FIGURE 9-6

To fix this, you need to implement the `area()` method in the `Rectangle` class:

```
class Rectangle: Shape {
    //---override the init() initializer---
    override init() {
        super.init()
    }

    //---overload the init() initializer---
    init(length:Double, width:Double) {
        super.init()
```

```
        self.length = length
        self.width = width
    }

    //---override the area() function---
    final override func area() -> Double {
        return self.length * self.width
    }
}
```

Observe that the `area()` method definition has two prefixes:

➤ `final`—The `final` keyword indicates that subclasses of `Rectangle` are not allowed to override the implementation of `area()`.

➤ `override`—Indicates that you are overriding the implementation of the `area()` method in the base class (`Shape`, that is)

You will now be able to use the `area()` method, as shown here:

```
rectangle.length = 5
rectangle.width = 6
println(rectangle.perimeter()) //---22---
println(rectangle.area())      //---30---
```

Overloading Methods

Besides overloading initializers, you can also overload methods. Using the `Shape` base class, the following creates another subclass called `Circle` that inherits from `Shape`:

```
class Circle: Shape {

    //---initializer---
    init(radius:Double) {
        super.init()
        self.width = radius * 2
        self.length = self.width
    }

    //---override the perimeter() function---
    override func perimeter() -> Double {
        return 2 * M_PI * (self.width/2)
    }

    //---overload the perimeter() function---
    func perimeter(#radius:Double) -> Double {

        //---adjust the length and width accordingly---
        self.length = radius * 2
        self.width = self.length

        return 2 * M_PI * radius
```

```
    }

    //---override the area() function---
    override func area() -> Double {
        return M_PI * pow(self.length / 2, 2)
    }
}
```

In the `Circle` class, you:

➤ have a new `init()` initializer

➤ override the `perimeter()` function in the base class

➤ overload the `perimeter()` function with one that accepts a radius argument

➤ override the `area()` function in the base class (`Shape`)

Figure 9-7 shows the class hierarchy of the `Circle` class.

You can now use the `Circle` class as follows:

FIGURE 9-7

```
var circle = Circle(radius: 6.8)
println(circle.perimeter())            // 42.7256600888212
println(circle.area())                 // 145.267244301992

//---need to specify the radius label---
println(circle.perimeter(radius:7.8))  // 49.0088453960008

//---call the perimter() method above
// changes the radius---
println(circle.area())                 // 191.134497044403
```

Because the `perimeter()` method is overloaded, you can call it either with no argument or with one argument (see Figure 9-8).

```
circle.perimeter()
M  Double perimeter()
M  Double perimeter(radius: Double)
```

FIGURE 9-8

Preventing Subclassing

So far, you have seen that both the `Circle` and the `Rectangle` class inherit from the `Shape` class. However, there are times when you want to prevent a class from being inherited. Consider the following `Square` class:

```
final class Square: Rectangle {
    //---overload the init() initializer---
    init(length:Double) {
        super.init()
```

```
        self.length = length
        self.width = self.length
    }
}
```

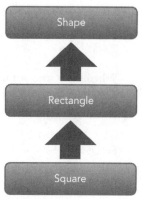

FIGURE 9-9

The `Square` class inherits from the `Rectangle` class (see Figure 9-9) and the class definition is prefixed with the `final` keyword. This indicates that no one other class can inherit from it. For example, the following is not allowed:

```
//---cannot inherit from Square as it is final---
class rhombus: Square {

}
```

In addition, because the `area()` method has been declared to be `final` in the `Rectangle` class, the `Square` class is not allowed to override it, as shown here:

```
final class Square: Rectangle {
    //---overload the init() initializer---
    init(length:Double) {
        super.init()
        self.length = length
        self.width = self.length
    }

    //---cannot override a final method---
    //---override the area() function---
    override func area() -> Double {
        ...
    }

}
```

TYPES OF INITIALIZERS

In the previous chapter on classes and structures, you learned about initializers. Initializers basically assign default values to the variables in your class so that they all have "initial" values when the class is instantiated. In Swift, there are three types of initializers:

➤ Default initializer

➤ Designated initializers

➤ Convenience initializers

Default Initializer

The *default initializer* is the initializer that is created by the compiler when your class is instantiated. For example, consider the following `Contact` class:

```
class Contact {
    var firstName:String = ""
```

```
    var lastName:String = ""
    var email:String = ""
    var group:Int = 0
}
```

When you create an instance of the `Contact` class, the compiler automatic generates a default initializer for the `Contact` class so that you can create the instance:

```
var c = Contact()
```

However, observe that all the stored properties in the `Contact` class are initialized to their default values. If they are not initialized to some values, such as the following, the compiler will complain that the class has no initializer:

```
class Contact {
    var firstName:String
    var lastName:String
    var email:String
    var group:Int
}
```

One way to fix this is to initialize each stored property (as we have done previously), or to explicitly create an initializer:

```
class Contact {
    var firstName:String
    var lastName:String
    var email:String
    var group:Int

    init() {
        firstName = ""
        lastName = ""
        email = ""
        group = 0
    }
}
```

In this case, you are creating your own initializer to initialize the values of the stored properties. This type of initializer is known as a *designated initializer*, which is discussed in the next section.

Designated Initializers

Sometimes you want to allow users of a class to pass in the values to initialize at the time of instantiation. In this case, you can create another initializer with parameters, as shown in the following example:

```
class Contact {
    var firstName:String
    var lastName:String
    var email:String
```

```
    var group:Int

    init() {
        firstName = ""
        lastName = ""
        email = ""
        group = 0
    }

    //---designated initializer---
    init(firstName: String, lastName:String, email:String, group: Int) {
        self.firstName = firstName
        self.lastName = lastName
        self.email = email
        self.group = group
    }
}
```

In the preceding example, the initializer is a *designated initializer,* as it initializes all the properties in the class. You can call the designated initializer as follows:

```
var c2 = Contact(
    firstName:"Wei-Meng",
    lastName:"Lee",
    email:"weimenglee@learn2develop.net",
    group:0)
```

Note that for initializers, you always have to label the various arguments passed into it, unless you write an underscore in front of the parameter name:

```
//---designated initializer---
init( _ firstName: String, _ lastName:String,
    _ email:String, _ group: Int) {
    self.firstName = firstName
    self.lastName = lastName
    self.email = email
    self.group = group
}
```

In this case, you can call the initializer without specifying the labels:

```
var c2 = Contact("Wei-Meng", "Lee",
                 "weimenglee@learn2develop.net",0)
```

A class is not limited to one designated initializer:

```
class Contact {
    var firstName:String
    var lastName:String
    var email:String
    var group:Int

    //---designated initializer---
    init() {
        firstName = ""
```

```
            lastName = ""
            email = ""
            group = 0
    }

    //---designated initializer---
    init(firstName: String, lastName:String, email:String, group: Int) {
        self.firstName = firstName
        self.lastName = lastName
        self.email = email
        self.group = group
    }

    //---designated initializer---
    init(firstName: String, lastName:String, email:String, group: Int,
    timeCreated:NSDate) {
        self.firstName = firstName
        self.lastName = lastName
        self.email = email
        self.group = group
        println(timeCreated)
    }

}
```

The preceding highlighted initializers are also designated initializers, as they initialize all the properties in the class.

Convenience Initializers and Initializer Chaining

The third type of initializer is known as a *convenience initializer.* To understand its use, consider the following example:

```
class Contact {
    var firstName:String
    var lastName:String
    var email:String
    var group:Int

    //---designated initializer---
    init() {
        firstName = ""
        lastName = ""
        email = ""
        group = 0
    }

    //---designated initializer---
    init(firstName: String, lastName:String, email:String, group: Int) {
        self.firstName = firstName
        self.lastName = lastName
        self.email = email
        self.group = group
```

```
    }

    //---designated initializer---
    init(firstName: String, lastName:String, email:String, group: Int,
    timeCreated:NSDate) {
        self.firstName = firstName
        self.lastName = lastName
        self.email = email
        self.group = group
        println(timeCreated)
    }

    //---convenience initializer; delegate to the designated one---
    convenience init(firstName: String, lastName:String, email:String) {
        self.init(firstName: firstName, lastName: lastName, email: email,
                group: 0)
    }

    //---convenience initializer; delegate to another convenience
    // initializer-
    convenience init(firstName: String, lastName:String) {
        self.init(firstName:firstName, lastName:lastName, email:"")
    }

    //---convenience initializer; delegate to another convenience
    // initializer---
    convenience init(firstName: String) {
        self.init(firstName:firstName, lastName:"")
    }

}
```

As Figure 9-10 illustrates, each convenience initializer calls another initializer. The convenience initializer with the fewest parameters calls the one with the next fewest number of parameters, and so on. This is call *initializer chaining*. Finally, the last convenience initializer calls the designated initializer.

delegate to the designated initializer

```
//---convenience initializer; delegate to the designated one---
convenience init(firstName: String, lastName:String, email:String) {
    self.init(firstName: firstName, lastName: lastName, email: email, group: 0)
}

//---convenience initializer; delegate to another convenience initializer---
convenience init(firstName: String, lastName:String) {
    self.init(firstName:firstName, lastName:lastName, email:"")
}

//---convenience initializer; delegate to another convenience initializer---
convenience init(firstName: String) {
    self.init(firstName:firstName, lastName:"")
}
```

FIGURE 9-10

Figure 9-11 shows that the `Contact` class now has six initializers.

```
    Contact()
 M  Contact ()
 M  Contact (firstName: String)
 M  Contact (firstName: String, lastName: String)
 M  Contact (firstName: String, lastName: String, email: String)
 M  Contact (firstName: String, lastName: String, email: String, group: Int)
 M  Contact (firstName: String, lastName: String, email: String, group: Int, timeCreated: NSDate)
```

FIGURE 9-11

Initializer chaining enables you to ensure that all properties in a class are fully initialized before use.

Calling Initializers in Subclasses

When a subclass inherits a base class and has its own initializer, you need to call the initializer in the base class. Consider the following example:

```
class Employee: Contact {
    init(firstName:String, lastName:String, email:String) {

    }
}
```

`Employee` inherits from the `Contact` base class and it overrides the initializers in `Contact`. In this case, you need to call the base class's initializer before you can do anything with the base class's properties. Trying to access any of the base class's properties will result in an error:

```
class Employee: Contact {

    init(firstName:String, lastName:String, email:String) {
        //---error---
        self.firstName = firstName
    }
}
```

However, you have to follow one rule: *The subclass can only call the base class's designated initializer.* The following will fail, as you are calling the base class's convenience initializer, not the designated initializer:

```
class Employee: Contact {
    init(firstName:String, lastName:String, email:String) {
        //---error; can only call designated initializer(s)---
        super.init(firstName: firstName, lastName: lastName, email: email)
    }
}
```

You need to call one of the base class's designated initializers:

```
class Employee: Contact {
    init(firstName:String, lastName:String, email:String) {
```

```
        super.init(firstName: firstName, lastName: lastName, email: email,
                group: 9)
    }
}
```

You can now create an instance of `Employee` as follows:

```
var e1 = Employee(firstName: "John", lastName: "Doe",
                email: "johndoe@example.com")
```

EXTENSIONS

Extensions in Swift enable you to add additional functionalities (such as methods) to an existing class.

> **NOTE** *Objective-C also supports extensions, except that it is called categories. Other languages that support extensions include C# and JavaScript.*

Extending Methods

To understand how extensions work, consider the following example:

```
extension String {
    func getLatLng(splitter:String) -> (Double, Double) {
        var latlng = self.componentsSeparatedByString(splitter)
        return ((latlng[0] as NSString).doubleValue,
                (latlng[1] as NSString).doubleValue)
    }
}
```

The preceding code snippet extends the `String` class with a method named `getLatLng()`. Its main function is to take in a string containing a latitude and longitude with a separator in between (say, a comma), and return a tuple containing the latitude and longitude in `Double` format. A sample string may look like this: "1.23456,103.345678." The `getLatLng()` method takes a `String` parameter (specifying the splitter between the latitude and longitude) and returns a tuple containing two `Doubles`.

To use the extension method, simply call it whenever you are dealing with a `String` variable or constant, as shown here:

```
var str = "1.23456,103.345678"
var latlng = str.getLatLng(",")
println(latlng.0)
println(latlng.1)
```

Extending Properties

Besides extending methods, extensions also work with properties, albeit only computed properties.

> **NOTE** *Extensions in Swift do not support stored properties.*

Remember the `Distance` class shown in the previous chapter:

```
class Distance {
    var miles = 0.0
    var km: Double {
        get {
            return 1.60934 * miles
        }
        set (km) {
            miles = km / 1.60934
        }
    }
}
```

You could extend the `Distance` class by adding computed properties to it:

```
extension Distance {
    var feet: Double { return miles * 5280 }
    var yard: Double { return miles * 1760 }
}
```

In the preceding code snippet, you added two new computed properties to the `Distance` class:

➤ `feet`—To convert the miles to feet

➤ `yard`—To convert the miles to yards

You can use the newly added computed properties as shown here:

```
var d = Distance()
d.miles = 10
println(d.feet)    //---52800.0---
println(d.yard)    //---17600.0---
```

ACCESS CONTROLS

In Swift, access control is modeled after the concept of modules and source files:

➤ **Module**—A single unit of distribution. The iPhone app that you developed and uploaded to the App Store as a single unit is a module. A framework that you package separately to be reused in different applications is also a module (see Figure 9-12). An application that uses another framework is considered to be two separate modules.

➤ **Source file**—A physical file within a module. For example, a source file may contain the definition of a single class, or, if you wish, the definition of multiple classes.

Module - App   **Module - Framework**

FIGURE 9-12

Swift's idea of access control is a little different from most other languages such as Java and C#. Most conventional OOP languages include three levels of scope:

➤ **Private scope**—Member variables are accessible within the class to which they are declared.

➤ **Protected scope**—Member variables are accessible within the class to which they are declared, as well as to subclasses.

➤ **Public scope**—Member variables are accessible to all code, inside or outside of the class in which they are declared.

Swift provides three different levels of access for your code, and these levels apply according to the location where an entity (constant, variable, class, property) is defined.

➤ **Public access**—The entity is accessible anywhere from within the file or module. You usually use public access for entities when you are writing a framework and exposing your APIs for public access.

➤ **Private access**—The entity is accessible only within the same physical file in which it is defined. For example, a variable declared as private in a class is still accessible to a subclass that is defined in the same physical file as the variable. If the subclass is defined in another physical file, the variable is not accessible.

➤ **Internal access**—By default, all entities defined in Swift have internal access, unless they are declared to be public or private. An entity that has internal access is accessible from within the physical file as well as within the same module the file belongs to.

Internal

Let's look at an example of how the various access control levels work. Assume that you have the following files:

➤ `ClassA.swift`

➤ `ClassB.swift`

`ClassA.swift` contains the following definition:

```
class ClassA {
    var a1 = 10
    //---same as---
    //internal var a1 = 10
}
```

`ClassB.swift` contains the following definition:

```
class ClassB {
    var b1 = 20
    //---same as---
    //internal var b1 = 20
}
```

By default, both `a1` and `b1` have `internal` access control. This means that as long as `ClassA.swift` and `ClassB.swift` are contained within the same module (see Figure 9.12 for examples of modules), `a1` is accessible by the code in `ClassB`, and `b1` is accessible by the code in `ClassA`. For example, suppose that `ClassA.swift` and `ClassB.swift` are both part of an iPhone application project. In this case, both `a1` and `b1` are accessible anywhere within the iPhone project.

Private

Using the same example, the following now adds the `private` keyword to both the declarations of `a1` and `b1`:

```
class ClassA {
    private var a1 = 10
}

class ClassB {
    private var b1 = 20
}
```

They will now be inaccessible outside the files. That is to say, `a1` is not accessible to the code in `ClassB`, and neither can the code in `ClassA` access `b1`.

If in `ClassA.swift` you now add another subclass that inherits from `ClassA`, then `a1` is still accessible:

```
//---these two classes within the same physical file---
class ClassA {
    private var a1 = 10
}

class SubclassA: ClassA {
    func doSomething() {
        self.a1 = 5
    }
}
```

In this case, a1 is still accessible within the same file in which it is declared, even though it is declared as `private`.

Public

If you want a1 (and b1) to be publicly accessible, you need to declare that using the `public` keyword:

```
class ClassA {
    public var a1 = 10
}
```

However, you will receive a compiler warning because `ClassA` has the default `internal` access, which essentially prevents a1 from being accessed outside the module. To fix this, make the class public as well:

```
public class ClassA {
    public var a1 = 10
}
```

The `ClassA` and its property a1 are now accessible outside the module.

SUMMARY

In this chapter, you learned how to declare a subclass that inherits from a base class. You also learned how to override and overload methods that are already defined in the current and parent class. In addition, you had a more detailed look at initializers and the different types of initializers you can create in a class. You also examined the rules that Swift adopts when calling initializers and how they behave in subclasses.

Another important topic covered in this chapter is extensions—a feature that enables you to extend functionalities to existing classes. Finally, you learned how Swift manages access controls and how they affect variable and constant accessibility in your application.

1. Create a `Vehicle` class that contains the following properties:

   ➤ `model`

   ➤ `doors`

   ➤ `color` – either red, blue, or white

   ➤ `wheels`

2. Create a subclass of `Vehicle` named `MotorVehicle`. Add an additional property to it named `licensePlate`.

3. Create a subclass of `Vehicle` named `Bicycle`.

4. Create a subclass of `MotorVehicle` named `Car`. Create the following initializers:

   ➤ an initializer that sets `doors` to 2

   ➤ an initializer that initializes the `model`, `doors`, `color`, and `wheels`

   ➤ a convenience initializer that initializes `licensePlate` and calls the initializer that initializes the `model`, `doors`, `color`, and `wheels`

▶ WHAT YOU LEARNED IN THIS CHAPTER

TOPIC	KEY CONCEPTS
Base class	A base class is simply a class that does not inherit from another class.
Abstract class	Swift does not officially support the concept of abstract classes; to implement them, you can improvise using a private initializer.
Class inheritance	To inherit from a base class, you create another class and specify the base class name after the colon (`:`).
Overriding base class initializer	When you override the base class initializer, you need to call the base class initializer using `super.init()`.
Overloading initializers	You can overload the initializers within a subclass. If a subclass does not have any initializers, then all the base class' initializers are available to the subclass. If a subclass has at least one initializer, then it will hide all the initializers in the base class.
Abstract methods	Swift does not support the concept of abstract methods. You can improvise abstract methods using the `assert()` function.
The `final` keyword	When applied to a method, the `final` keyword indicates that subclasses of the current class are not allowed to override the particular method. When applied to a class, this means that the current class cannot be subclassed by another class.
Types of initializers	There are three types of initializers: default, designated, and convenience.
Calling initializers in subclasses	A subclass can call only the base class's designated initializer, not the convenience initializer's.
Extensions	Extensions enable you to add functionalities (such as methods) to an existing class.
Access controls	Swift provides three different levels of access: `public`, `private`, and `internal`.
Public access	The entity is accessible anywhere from within the file or module. You usually use public access for entities when you are writing a framework and exposing your APIs for public access.
Private access	The entity is accessible only within the same physical file in which it is defined. For example, a variable declared as private in a class is still accessible to a subclass that is defined in the same physical file as the variable. If the subclass is defined in another physical file, the variable is not accessible.
Internal access	By default, all entities defined in Swift have internal access, unless they are declared to be public or private. An entity that has internal access is accessible from within the physical file as well as within the same module to which the file belongs.

10

Closures

WHAT YOU WILL LEARN IN THIS CHAPTER:

➤ What closures are

➤ Functions as special types of closures

➤ How to create a closure as a variable

➤ How to write a closure inline

➤ How to simplify closures using type inference

➤ How to simplify closures using shorthand argument names

➤ How to simplify closures using operator functions

➤ How to write a trailing closure

➤ How to use the `Array`'s three closure functions: `map()`, `filter()`, and `reduce()`

➤ How to declare and use closures in your functions

One of the important features in Swift is the *closure*. Closures are self-contained blocks of code that can be passed to functions to be executed as independent code units. Think of a closure as a function without a name. In fact, functions are actually special cases of closures.

Swift offers various ways to optimize closures so that they are brief and succinct. The various optimizations include the following:

➤ Inferring parameter types and return type

➤ Implicit returns from single-statement closures

➤ Shorthand argument names

➤ Trailing closure syntax

➤ Operator closure

> **NOTE** *Closure is Swift's answer to Objective-C's block syntax and C#'s Lambda expressions.*

UNDERSTANDING CLOSURES

The best way to understand closures is to use an example. Suppose you have the following array of integers:

```
let numbers = [5,2,8,7,9,4,3,1]
```

Assume you want to sort this array in ascending order. You could write your own function to perform the sorting, or you could use the sorted() function available in Swift. The sorted() function takes two arguments:

➤ An array to be sorted

➤ A *closure* that takes two arguments of the same type as the array, and returns a true if the first value should appear before the second value

Functions as Closures

In Swift, functions are special types of closures. As mentioned in the previous section, the sorted() function needs a closure that takes two arguments of the same type as the array, returning a true if the first value should appear before the second value. The following function fulfills that requirement:

```
func ascending(num1:Int, num2:Int) -> Bool {
    return num1<num2
}
```

The ascending() function takes two arguments of type Int and returns a Bool value. If num1 is less than num2, it returns true. You can now pass this function to the sorted() function, as shown here:

```
var sortedNumbers = sorted(numbers, ascending)
```

The sorted() function will now return the array that is sorted in ascending order. You can verify this by outputting the values in the array:

```
println("===Unsorted===")
println(numbers)

println("===Sorted===")
println(sortedNumbers)
```

The preceding statements output the following:

```
===Unsorted===
[5, 2, 8, 7, 9, 4, 3, 1]
===Sorted===
[1, 2, 3, 4, 5, 7, 8, 9]
```

> **NOTE** The `sorted()` *function does not modify the original array. It returns the sorted array as a new array.*

Assigning Closures to Variables

As mentioned earlier, functions are special types of closures. In fact, a closure is a function without a name. However, you can assign a closure to a variable—for example, the `ascending()` function discussed earlier can be written as a closure assigned to a variable:

```
var compareClosure : (Int, Int)->Bool =
{
    (num1:Int, num2:Int) -> Bool in
        return num1 < num2
}
```

The preceding code snippet first declares that it is a closure that takes two `Int` arguments and returns a `Bool` value:

```
var compareClosure : (Int, Int)->Bool =
```

The actual implementation of the closure is then defined:

```
{
    (num1:Int, num2:Int) -> Bool in
        return num1 < num2
}
```

To use the `compareClosure` closure with the `sorted()` function, pass in the `compareClosure` variable:

```
var sortedNumbers = sorted(numbers, compareClosure)
```

In general, a closure has the following syntax:

```
{
    ([parameters]) -> [return type] in
        [statements]
}
```

Writing Closures Inline

While an earlier section showed how to pass a function into the `sorted()` function as a closure function, a better way is to write the closure *inline*, which obviates the need to define a function explicitly or assign it to a variable.

Rewriting the earlier example would yield the following:

```
var sortedNumbers = sorted(numbers,
    {
        (num1:Int, num2:Int) -> Bool in
            return num1<num2
    }
)
```

As you can observe, the `ascending()` function name is now gone; all you have supplied is the parameter list and the content of the function.

If you want to sort the array in descending order, you can simply change the comparison operator:

```
var sortedNumbers = sorted(numbers,
    {
        (num1:Int, num2:Int) -> Bool in
        return num1>num2
    }
)
println("===Sorted===")
println(sortedNumbers)
```

The array will now be sorted in descending order:

```
===Sorted===
[9, 8, 7, 5, 4, 3, 2, 1]
```

If you want to sort a list of strings, you can write your closure as follows:

```
var fruits = ["orange", "apple", "durian", "rambutan", "pineapple"]

println(sorted(fruits,
    {
        (fruit1:String, fruit2:String) -> Bool in
            return fruit1<fruit2
    })
)
```

The output is as shown:

```
[apple, durian, orange, pineapple, rambutan]
```

Type Inference

Because the type of the first argument of the closure function must be the same as the type of array you are sorting, it is actually redundant to specify the type in the closure, as the compiler can infer that from the type of array you are using:

```
var fruits = ["orange", "apple", "durian", "rambutan", "pineapple"]
println(sorted(fruits,
    {
        (fruit1:String, fruit2:String) -> Bool in
            return fruit1<fruit2
    })
)
```

The preceding could be rewritten without specifying the type:

```
println(sorted(fruits,
    {
        (fruit1, fruit2) in
            return fruit1<fruit2
    })
)
```

If your closure has only a single statement, you can even omit the `return` keyword:

```
println(sorted(fruits,
    {
        (fruit1, fruit2) in
            fruit1<fruit2
    })
)
```

Shorthand Argument Names

In the previous section, names were given to arguments within a closure. In fact, this is also optional, as Swift automatically provides shorthand names to the parameters, which you can refer to as $0, $1, and so on.

The previous code snippet:

```
println(sorted(fruits,
    {
        (fruit1, fruit2) in
            fruit1<fruit2
    })
)
```

could be rewritten as follows without using named parameters:

```
println(sorted(fruits,
    {
        $0<$1
    })
)
```

To make the closure really terse, you can write everything on one line:

```
println(sorted(fruits, { $0<$1 }))
```

Operator Function

In the previous section you saw that the closure for the `sorted()` function was reduced to the following:

```
println(sorted(fruits, { $0<$1 }))
```

One of the implementations of the lesser than (<) operator is actually a function that works with two operands of type `String`. Because of this, you can actually simply specify the < operator in place of the closure, and the compiler will automatically infer that you want to use the particular implementation of the < operator. The preceding statement can be reduced to the following:

```
println(sorted(fruits, <))
```

If you want to sort the array in descending order, simply use the greater than (>) operator:

```
println(sorted(fruits, >))
```

Trailing Closures

Consider the closure that you saw earlier:

```
println(sorted(fruits,
    {
        (fruit1:String, fruit2:String) -> Bool in
            return fruit1<fruit2
    })
)
```

Observe that the closure is passed in as a second argument of the `sorted()` function. For long closures, this syntax might be a little messy. If the closure is the final argument of a function, you can rewrite this closure as a *trailing closure*. A trailing closure is written outside of the parentheses of the function call. The preceding code snippet when rewritten using the trailing closure looks like this:

```
println(sorted(fruits)
    {
        (fruit1:String, fruit2:String) -> Bool in
        return fruit1<fruit2
    }
)
```

Using the shorthand argument name, the closure can be shortened to the following:

```
println(sorted(fruits) { $0<$1 })
```

USING THE ARRAY'S THREE CLOSURE FUNCTIONS

The `Array` structure in Swift is a good example for examining how closure works. It has three built-in methods that accept closures as part of the argument list:

➤   `map()`—Enables you to transform the elements inside an array into another array

➤ `filter()`—Enables you to filter the elements inside an array and return a subset of the elements

➤ `reduce()`—Enables you to return the elements inside an array as a single item

The map Function

In Swift, `Array` supports the `map()` function, which enables you to transform the elements from one array into another array.

For the following examples, assume you have an array that contains the prices of some items:

```
let prices = [12.0,45.0,23.5,78.9,12.5]
```

Example 1

Suppose you want to transform the `prices` array into another array with each element containing the dollar ($) sign, like this:

```
["$12.0", "$45.0", "$23.5", "$78.9", "$12.5"]
```

Instead of iterating through the original `prices` array and creating another one manually by copying each element, the `map()` function enables you to do it easily. Consider the following code snippet:

```
var pricesIn$ = prices.map(
    {
        (price:Double) -> String in
            return "$\(price)"
    }
)

println(pricesIn$)
```

The `map()` function accepts a closure as its argument. The closure itself accepts a single argument representing each element of the original array, and in this example the closure returns a `String` result. The closure is called once for every element in the array.

In the preceding implementation, you simply prefix each price with the $ sign. The resultant array is assigned to `pricesIn$` and it now contains an array of `String` type:

```
[$12.0, $45.0, $23.5, $78.9, $12.5]
```

Based on the earlier discussion about type inference, the preceding code can be reduced to the following:

```
let prices = [12.0,45.0,23.5,78.9,12.5]

var pricesIn$ = prices.map(
    {
        (price) -> String in
            "$\(price)"
    }
)

println(pricesIn$)
```

Using the shorthand argument names, and because the closure has only a single line, the code can be further reduced as follows:

```
var pricesIn$ = prices.map(
    {
        "$\($0)"
    }
)
```

Example 2

Instead of prefixing each price with the $ sign, you might want to apply a GST (goods and services tax) to each item so that the price is inclusive of GST. Furthermore, assume that the GST is applied only to prices above 20 and that the GST rate is 7 percent.

The code to apply a GST to the array looks like the following:

```
var pricesWithGST = prices.map(
    {
        (price:Double) -> Double in
            if price > 20 {
                return price * 1.07
            } else {
                return price
            }
    }
)
println(pricesWithGST)
```

In this example, the closure accepts the price as the argument and returns a Double result. Each price that is greater than 20 is multiplied by 1.07. The preceding code will output the following:

```
[12.0, 48.15, 25.145, 84.423, 12.5]
```

Applying type inherence and using the ternary operator, the code can now be reduced to this:

```
var pricesWithGST = prices.map(
    {
        (price) in
            price>20 ? price * 1.07 : price
    }
)
```

The filter Function

The filter() function returns another array containing a subset of the original elements that satisfy the specified criteria.

Example 1

Using the same prices array, the following code snippet shows how to apply a filter to the array to return all those elements greater than 20:

```
let prices = [12.0,45.0,23.5,78.9,12.5]
var pricesAbove20 = prices.filter(
    {
        (price:Double) -> Bool in
            price>20
    }
)
println(pricesAbove20)
```

Like the map() function, the filter() function takes a closure. The closure itself accepts a single argument representing each element of the original array, and returns a Bool result. The closure is called once for every element in the array. The result will contain the element if the statement (price>20) evaluates to true.

The preceding code snippet outputs the following:

```
[45.0, 23.5, 78.9]
```

Using type inference, the code can be reduced as follows:

```
var pricesAbove20 = prices.filter(
    {
        (price) in
            price>20
    }
)
```

Eliminating the named parameters yields this:

```
var pricesAbove20 = prices.filter({ $0>20 })
```

Example 2

Suppose you have the following array of names:

```
let names = ["Davi", "Jacob", "Nathan", "Pedro", "Mason",
             "Carter", "Jayden", "Ryan"]
```

Now assume you want to extract all the names that contain the word "an." You can use the filter() function with the following closure:

```
var someNames = names.filter(
    {
        (name:String) in
            (name as NSString).containsString("an")
    }
)
println(someNames)
```

Each name in the names array is passed into the closure and type-casted into an NSString object. You can call the containsString() method to test whether the name contains the word "an."

The preceding code snippet outputs the following line:

```
[Nathan, Ryan]
```

Using type inference, the closure looks like this:

```
var someNames = names.filter(
    {
        (name) in
            (name as NSString).containsString("an")
    }
)
```

Using shorthand argument naming, the closure can be reduced to the following:

```
var someNames = names.filter(
    {
        ($0 as NSString).containsString("an")
    }
)
```

The reduce Function

The reduce() function returns a single value representing the result of applying a reduction closure to the elements in the array.

Example 1

Using the same prices array, the following code snippet shows how to sum all the prices in the array:

```
let prices = [12.0,45.0,23.5,78.9,12.5]
var totalPrice =  prices.reduce(
    0.0,
    {
        (subTotal: Double, price: Double) -> Double in
            return subTotal + price
    }
)
println(totalPrice)
```

The reduce() function takes two arguments:

➤ **The initial value for the result**—In this example, 0.0 is initially assigned to subtotal.

➤ **A closure that takes two arguments**—The first argument takes the initial value (in this case, 0.0), and the second argument takes the first element in the array. The closure is called recursively and the result passed in to the same closure as the first argument, and the next element in the array is passed in as the second argument. This happens until the last element in the array is processed.

The closure recursively sums up all the prices in the array and outputs the following result:

```
171.9
```

Applying type inference reduces the closure to the following:

```
var totalPrice =  prices.reduce(
    0.0,
```

```
    {
        (subTotal, price) in
            return subTotal + price
    }
)
```

Removing the named parameters yields the following closure:

```
var totalPrice =  prices.reduce(0.0, { $0 + $1 })
println(totalPrice)
```

Using an operator function, the closure can be further reduced:

```
var totalPrice =  prices.reduce(0.0,  + )
```

Example 2

Suppose you want to extract all the prices from the array and create a single string listing all of them. You can write the following closure:

```
let prices = [12.0,45.0,23.5,78.9,12.5]
var allPrices =  prices.reduce(
    "List of prices",
    {
        (subString: String, price: Double) -> String in
            return ("\(subString)\n$\(price)")
    }
)
println(allPrices)
```

The preceding code snippet will output the following:

```
List of prices
$12.0
$45.0
$23.5
$78.9
$12.5
```

Using type inference, the closure now looks like this:

```
var allPrices =  prices.reduce(
    "List of prices",
    {
        (subString, price) in
            "\(subString)\n$\(price)"
    }
)
```

Removing the named parameters further reduces the closure as follows:

```
var allPrices =  prices.reduce(
    "List of prices", { "\($0)\n$\($1)" })
```

USING CLOSURES IN YOUR FUNCTIONS

So far, in the earlier sections you have seen how to use closures in functions. What about declaring your own functions to use closures? Suppose you have a function that performs a bubble sort:

```
func bubbleSort(inout items:[Int])  {
    for var j=0; j<items.count-1; j++ {
        var swapped = false
        for var i=0; i<items.count-1-j; i++ {
            if items[i] > items[i+1] {
                var temp = items[i+1]
                items[i+1] = items[i]
                items[i] = temp
                swapped = true
            }
        }
        if !swapped {
            break
        }
    }
}
```

The `bubbleSort()` function sorts an array of `Int` values in ascending order like this:

```
var numbers = [6,7,8,9,2,1,3,4,5]
bubbleSort(&numbers)
println(numbers)  //---[1, 2, 3, 4, 5, 6, 7, 8, 9]---
```

The `bubbleSort()` function is hardcoded to sort the numbers in ascending order. If you want to sort the numbers in descending order, you have to change its comparison operator:

```
func bubbleSort(inout items:[Int])  {
    for var j=0; j<items.count-1; j++ {
        var swapped = false
        for var i=0; i<items.count-1-j; i++ {
            if items[i] < items[i+1] {
                var temp = items[i+1]
                items[i+1] = items[i]
                items[i] = temp
                swapped = true
            }
        }
        if !swapped {
            break
        }
    }
}
```

Creating different functions to sort in a different order is not a good design. A better way would be to let the caller decide the sorting order. This is where closure shines.

Consider the following condition:

```
if items[i] < items[i+1] {
```

You can probably see that it can be replaced with a function, such as this:

```
if compareFunction(items[i], items[i+1]) {
```

The compareFunction() function takes two Int arguments and returns a Bool value and thus it has the following function type:

```
(Int, Int) -> Bool
```

This is a good opportunity to use closure so that the actual comparison of the numbers can be left to the caller of this bubbleSort() function. When the bubbleSort() function is updated to use closure, it looks like this:

```
func bubbleSort(inout items: [Int], compareFunction:(Int, Int)->Bool) {
    for var j=0; j<items.count-1; j++ {
        var swapped = false
        for var i=0; i<items.count-1-j; i++ {
            if compareFunction(items[i],items[i+1]) {
                var temp = items[i+1]
                items[i+1] = items[i]
                items[i] = temp
                swapped = true
            }
        }
        if !swapped {
            break
        }
    }
}
```

To sort in descending order, simply pass in a closure like this:

```
bubbleSort(&numbers,
    {
        (num1:Int, num2:Int) -> Bool in
            return num1 < num2
    }
)
```

To sort in ascending order, simply pass in a closure like this:

```
bubbleSort(&numbers,
    {
        (num1:Int, num2:Int) -> Bool in
            return num1 > num2
    }
)
```

When you apply type inference and remove the named argument, you can reduce the preceding code to the following:

```
bubbleSort(&numbers, { $0 > $1 })
```

SUMMARY

In this chapter, you learned about the Swift concept known as a closure. The closure is not really new to Objective-C programmers, as it appeared in the form of blocks. You can assign closures to variables, pass them as arguments to functions, as well as write them inline. Closures provide a lot of flexibility, as they enable callers of your app to pass in their own self-defined functions. Using type inference, shorthand argument names, and trailing closures, there are many ways to write extremely terse closures. In your implementation, it is always important to strike a balance between code readability and code efficiency.

EXERCISES

1. Given an array of single-digit integers, write the code snippet to return the English equivalent of each integer:

   ```
   var numbers = [5,6,3,2,4,8,1,0]
   //---should output:
   // [Five, Six, Three, Two, Four, Eight, One, Zero]
   ```

2. Write the code snippet to extract only the odd numbers from the array shown in question #1.

3. Write the code snippet to find out the largest number from the array shown in question #1.

4. Write the code snippet to find out the average of all the numbers from the array shown in question #1.

▶ **WHAT YOU LEARNED IN THIS CHAPTER**

TOPIC	KEY CONCEPTS
Closures	Closures are self-contained blocks of code that can be passed to functions to be executed as independent code units.
Functions as closures	Functions are special types of closures. A closure is a function without a name.
Shorthand argument names in a closure	You can refer to the arguments within a closure as $0, $1, and so on.
`Array`'s three closure functions	The three closure functions are `map()`, `filter()`, and `reduce()`.
The `map()` function	Enables you to transform the elements from one array into another array.
The `filter()` function	Returns another array containing a subset of the original elements that satisfy the specified criteria.
The `reduce()` function	Returns a single value representing the result of applying a reduction closure to the elements in the array.

11

Protocols and Delegates

WHAT YOU WILL LEARN IN THIS CHAPTER:

- ➤ What a protocol is
- ➤ How to define and use a protocol
- ➤ How to conform to a protocol
- ➤ How to declare optional methods in a protocol
- ➤ How to conform to multiple protocols
- ➤ How to specify property requirements in a protocol
- ➤ How to specify initializer requirements in a protocol
- ➤ What a delegate is
- ➤ How to create and use a delegate
- ➤ How protocols and delegates are used in real-life apps

WROX.COM CODE DOWNLOADS FOR THIS CHAPTER

The code downloads for this chapter are found at www.wrox.com/go/beginningswift on the Download Code tab.

The use of protocols and delegates reflects one of the most important design patterns in Swift programming. In Chapters 8 and 9 you have seen how classes and inheritance work; and in this chapter, you will learn both how to use protocols to enforce the content of a class and how delegates help to create events and event handlers.

UNDERSTANDING PROTOCOLS

A *protocol* is a blueprint of methods and properties. It describes what a class should have, and it does not provide any implementation. A class that *conforms* to a protocol needs to provide the implementation as dictated by the protocol. A protocol can be implemented by a class, a structure, or an enumeration.

> **NOTE** *A protocol is similar to what an interface is in Java.*

Defining and Using a Protocol

To define a protocol, use the `protocol` keyword, followed by the name of the protocol:

```
protocol ProtocolName {
    func method1()
    func method2()
    ...
}
```

> **NOTE** *Methods in a protocol follow the same syntax as normal methods in a class, with only one exception: You are not allowed to specify default values for method parameters.*

Here is an example of a protocol:

```
protocol CarProtocol {
    func accelerate()
    func decelerate()
}
```

The preceding code snippet declares a protocol named `CarProtocol` containing two methods: `accelerate()` and `decelerate()`. A class that wants to implement a car that can accelerate or decelerate can *conform* to this protocol.

Conforming to a Protocol

To conform to a protocol, specify the protocol name(s) after the class name, as shown here:

```
class ClassName: ProtocolName1, ProtocolName2 {
    ...
}
```

If you are conforming to more than one protocol, separate them using a comma (,). If your class is also extending from another class, specify the protocol name(s) after the class it is extending:

```
class ClassName: BaseClass, ProtocolName1, ProtocolName2 {
    ...
}
```

The following code snippet shows an example of how to conform to a protocol:

```
class Car: CarProtocol {
    ...
}
```

In the preceding code snippet, the Car class is said to "*conform to the* CarProtocol." Any class that conforms to the CarProtocol must implement the methods declared in it.

To conform to the CarProtocol protocol, the Car class might look like this:

```
class Car: CarProtocol {
    var speed = 0

    func accelerate() {
        speed += 10
        if speed > 50 {
            speed = 50
        }
        printSpeed()
    }

    func decelerate() {
        speed -= 10
        if speed<=0 {
            speed = 0
        }
        printSpeed()
    }

    func stop() {
        while speed>0 {
            decelerate()
        }
    }

    func printSpeed() {
        println("Speed: \(speed)")
    }
}
```

Note that in addition to implementing the accelerate() and decelerate() methods that are declared in CarProtocol, the Car class is free to implement other methods as required—in this case it also implements the `stop()` and `printSpeed()` methods. If any of the methods declared in `CarProtocol` are not implemented in the `Car` class, the compiler will flag an error (see Figure 11-1).

```
class Car: CarProtocol  {
                          Type 'Car' does not conform to protocol 'CarProtocol'



}
```

FIGURE 11-1

You can now create an instance of the `Car` class and call its various methods to accelerate the car, decelerate it, as well as make it come to a stop:

```
var c1 = Car()
c1.accelerate()   //---Speed: 10---
c1.accelerate()   //---Speed: 20---
c1.accelerate()   //---Speed: 30---
c1.accelerate()   //---Speed: 40---
c1.accelerate()   //---Speed: 50---
c1.decelerate()   //---Speed: 40---
c1.stop()         //---Speed: 30---
                  //---Speed: 20---
                  //---Speed: 10---
                  //---Speed: 0---
```

Optional Methods

In the previous section, the `CarProtocol` contains two methods that are mandatory for classes that conform to the protocol to implement. However, sometimes you want to provide the option for the implementing class to determine whether it will implement a particular method. You can do so by specifying a method within a protocol as an *optional method* using the `optional` keyword.

The following code snippet shows the `CarProtocol` now has an optional method called `accelerateBy()`:

```
@objc protocol CarProtocol {
    func accelerate()
    func decelerate()
    optional func accelerateBy(amount:Int)
}
```

Note the use of the `@objc` tag prefixing the `protocol` keyword. The `@objc` tag indicates to the compiler that your class is interoperating with Objective-C. You need to prefix the protocol with this tag in order to declare optional methods in your protocol, even if you do not intend to use your class with Objective-C code. All optional methods are prefixed with the `optional` keyword.

> **NOTE** *Protocols that are prefixed with the* `@objc` *tag can only be applied to classes, not structures and enumerations.*

In the `Car` class, you can now choose to implement the optional `accelerateBy()` method if desired:

```
class Car: CarProtocol {
    var speed = 0

    func accelerate() {
        speed += 10
        if speed > 50 {
            speed = 50
        }
        printSpeed()
    }

    func decelerate() {
        speed -= 10
        if speed<=0 {
            speed = 0
        }
        printSpeed()
    }

    func stop() {
        while speed>0 {
            decelerate()
        }
    }

    func printSpeed() {
        println("Speed: \(speed)")
    }

    func accelerateBy(amount:Int) {
        speed += amount
        if speed > 50 {
            speed = 50
        }
        printSpeed()
    }
}
```

The following example shows how you can use the `accelerateBy()` method in your class:

```
var c1 = Car()
c1.accelerate()    //---Speed: 10---
c1.accelerate()    //---Speed: 20---
```

```
c1.accelerate()    //---Speed: 30---
c1.accelerate()    //---Speed: 40---
c1.accelerate()    //---Speed: 50---
c1.decelerate()    //---Speed: 40---
c1.stop()          //---Speed: 30---
                   //---Speed: 20---
                   //---Speed: 10---
                   //---Speed: 0---
c1.accelerateBy(5) //---Speed: 5---
c1.accelerateBy(5) //---Speed: 10---
```

Conforming to Multiple Protocols

A class can conform to multiple protocols. Suppose there is another protocol called
CarDetailsProtocol. If the Car class should conform to both the CarProtocol as well as the
CarDetailsProtocol, then you separate the two protocols with a comma (,):

```
@objc class Car: CarProtocol, CarDetailsProtocol {

    ...

}
```

Property Requirements

Besides specifying methods to implement, a protocol can also specify properties that a confirming
class needs to implement. As an example, consider the following CarDetailsProtocol:

```
protocol CarDetailsProtocol {
    var model: String {get set}
    var doors: Int {get set}
    var currentSpeed: Int {get}
}
```

The CarDetailsProtocol protocol specifies three properties that need to be implemented. It does
not specify whether you need to implement stored or computed properties; it just specifies the name
and type, as well as whether each property is *settable* or *gettable*. It is up to the implementing class
to decide how to implement the properties.

The following code snippet shows the Car class conforming to the CarDetailsProtocol:

```
@objc class Car: CarProtocol, CarDetailsProtocol {
    var speed = 0

    var model: String = ""
    var doors: Int = 0

    var currentSpeed: Int {
        return speed
    }

    func accelerate() {
        ...
```

```
    }

    . . .

}
```

Here, you can see that both the `model` and `doors` properties are implemented as stored properties. The `currentSpeed` property is implemented as a read-only computed property, as it is specified as only *gettable* in the protocol.

Initializer Requirements

You can also enforce a class to implement an initializer using a protocol. Using the `CarDetailsProtocol` example, you can now enforce that a conforming class implements the initializer as follows:

```
protocol CarDetailsProtocol {
    init(model:String)

    var model: String {get set}
    var doors: Int {get set}
    var currentSpeed: Int {get}
}
```

Therefore, for the `Car` class, if it now conforms to the `CarDetailsProtocol`, it needs to implement the initializer:

```
@objc class Car: CarProtocol, CarDetailsProtocol {
    var speed = 0
    var model: String = ""
    var doors: Int = 0

    required init(model:String) {
        self.model = model
    }

    var currentSpeed: Int {
        return speed
    }
```

You need the `required` keyword to ensure that subclasses of `Car` also provide an implementation for the initializer.

UNDERSTANDING DELEGATES

A delegate is an instance of a type (such as a class) that can handle the methods of a class or a structure. Think of a delegate as an *event handler.* A class or structure can fire events, and it needs *something* to handle these events. In this case, the class or structure can "delegate" this task to an instance of a type. This instance of a type is the delegate.

Delegates as Event Handlers

Let's look at a concrete example to drive home the point. In the previous section, you saw the `Car` class has implemented the following methods as declared in the `CarProtocol`:

➤ `accelerate()`—Accelerates the car by 10 mph

➤ `decelerate()`—Decelerates the car by 10 mph

➤ `accelerateBy()`—Accelerates the car by the amount specified in the argument

If the car has reached its maximum speed, it is important that the class fires an event to let the user of the class know. Similarly, if the car has come to a complete stop, it is also important to let the user know. It is also useful to notify the user whenever the car is accelerating or decelerating. All the preceding behaviors of the class can be implemented as a protocol:

```
@objc protocol CarDelegate {
    func reachedMaxSpeed(c: Car)
    func completelyStopped(c: Car)

    optional func accelerating(c: Car)
    optional func decelerating(c: Car)
}
```

In the preceding code snippet, `CarDelegate` is a protocol that contains four methods—two mandatory and two optional. Each method takes a `Car` argument:

➤ `reachedMaxSpeed()`—Fired when the car has reached maximum speed

➤ `completelyStopped()`—Fired when the car comes to a complete stop

➤ `accelerating()`—Fired when the car is accelerating

➤ `decelerating()`—Fired when the car is decelerating

> **NOTE** *Think of the four methods as events.*

To make use of the `CarDelegate`, add the following code in bold to the `Car` class:

```
@objc class Car: CarProtocol {
    var delegate: CarDelegate?
    var speed = 0
    func accelerate() {
        speed += 10
        if speed > 50 {
            speed = 50
            //---call the reachedMaxSpeed() declared
            // in the CarDelegate ---
            delegate?.reachedMaxSpeed(self)
```

```
        } else {
            //---call the accelerating() declared
            // in the CarDelegate ---
            delegate?.accelerating?(self)
        }
        printSpeed()
    }

    func decelerate()   {
        speed -= 10
        if speed<=0 {
            speed = 0
            //---call the completelyStopped() declared in
            // the CarDelegate---
            delegate?.completelyStopped(self)
        } else {
            //---call the decelerating() declared
            // in the CarDelegate ---
            delegate?.decelerating?(self)
        }
        printSpeed()
    }

    func stop() {
        while speed>0 {
            decelerate()
        }
    }

    func printSpeed() {
        println("Speed: \(speed)")
    }

    func accelerateBy(amount:Int) {
        speed += amount
        if speed > 50 {
            speed = 50
            //---call the reachedMaxSpeed() declared in
            // the CarDelegate---
            delegate?.reachedMaxSpeed(self)
        } else {
            //---call the accelerating() declared
            // in the CarDelegate ---
            delegate?.accelerating?(self)
        }
        printSpeed()
    }
}
```

Here is what you are doing:

> ➤ You first declare a variable called `delegate` of type `CarDelegate`. You need the `?` sign to indicate to the compiler that this `delegate` variable is an optional variable (may be nil). This `delegate` variable can be assigned an instance of a class that implements the `CarDelegate` protocol. You will see how this is done shortly.

➤ If the speed of the car is more than 50 mph, limit it to 50 mph, then use the delegate variable and call the `reachedMaxSpeed()` method. Recall that the `delegate` variable is set to an instance of a class that implements the `CarDelegate` protocol; hence the instance must have the `reachedMaxSpeed()` method defined. The `?` is to check whether the `delegate` variable is set (not `nil`):

```
delegate?.reachedMaxSpeed(self)
```

> **NOTE** Because `delegate` *is an optional type, using* `?` *will prevent the code from crashing if* `delegate` *is* `nil`*. If the value is* `nil`*, calling the* `reachedMaxSpeed()` *method has no effect. If you use the* `!` *to wrap the optional value, the statement will crash if* `delegate` *is* `nil`*.*

➤ When the car is accelerating, you use the `delegate` variable and call the `accelerating()` method. Because the `accelerating()` method is an optional method as declared in the `CarDelegate` protocol, you therefore have to use the `?` after the method name to check whether the method is implemented in the instance:

```
delegate?.accelerating?(self)
```

➤ You do the same for the `completelyStopped()` and the `decelerating()` methods:

```
delegate?.completelyStopped(self)
delegate?.decelerating?(self)
```

➤ You need to prefix the `Car` class with the `@objc` tag because the methods in the `CarDelegate` protocol contain references to the `Car` class.

Now that you have modified the `Car` class to have a variable of type `CarDelegate`, we can create a class that implements the `CarDelegate` protocol. The following `CarStatus` class conforms to the `CarDelegate` protocol:

```
class CarStatus: CarDelegate {
    func reachedMaxSpeed(c: Car) {
        println("Car has reached max speed! Speed is \(c.speed)mph")
    }

    func completelyStopped(c: Car) {
        println("Car has completely stopped! Speed is \(c.speed)mph")
    }

    //===optional methods===

    func accelerating(c: Car) {
        println("Car is accelerating...Speed is \(c.speed)mph")
    }
```

```
    func decelerating(c: Car) {
        println("Car is decelerating...Speed is \(c.speed)mph")
    }
}
```

The CarStatus class implements the four methods as declared in the CarDelegate protocol, two of which are optional.

> **NOTE** *Think of the* CarStatus *class as the event handler for the* Car *class.*

You can now create an instance of the CarStatus class and assign it to the delegate property of the Car class:

```
var c1 = Car(model: "F150")
c1.delegate = CarStatus()
c1.accelerate()   //---Car is accelerating...Speed is 10mph---
                  //---Speed: 10---
c1.accelerate()   //---Car is accelerating...Speed is 20mph---
                  //---Speed: 20---
c1.accelerate()   //---Car is accelerating...Speed is 30mph---
                  //---Speed: 30---
c1.accelerate()   //---Car is accelerating...Speed is 40mph---
                  //---Speed: 40---
c1.accelerate()   //---Car is accelerating...Speed is 50mph---
                  //---Speed: 50---
c1.accelerate()   //---Car has reached max speed! Speed is 50mph---
                  //---Speed: 50---
c1.stop()         //---Car is decelerating...Speed is 40mph---
                  //---Speed: 40---
                  //---Car is decelerating...Speed is 30mph---
                  //---Speed: 30---
                  //---Car is decelerating...Speed is 20mph---
                  //---Speed: 20---
                  //---Car is decelerating...Speed is 10mph---
                  //---Speed: 10---
                  //---Car has completely stopped! Speed is 0mph---
                  //---Speed: 0---
```

As you call the various methods of the Car instance, the various methods in the CarDelegate protocol will be fired and the result printed on the screen, as shown in the preceding code snippet.

A Practical Example of Protocols and Delegates

To see how protocols and delegates work in the iOS design pattern grand scheme of things, this section examines how it is used to help you obtain location information.

In iOS, the `CLLocationManager` class (Location Manager) helps you find the location of the device. To use the `CLLocationManager` class, create an instance of it—say, in your View Controller:

```
import CoreLocation

class ViewController: UIViewController {
    var lm: CLLocationManager!
```

You then configure the instance of the `CLLocationManager` class; in particular, you set its `delegate` property:

```
lm = CLLocationManager()
lm.delegate = self
lm.desiredAccuracy = 0
lm.distanceFilter = 0
```

When you set the `delegate` property to `self`, it means that the class containing the `lm` variable needs to conform to the protocol dictated by the `CLLocationManager` class, which in this case is `CLLocationManagerDelegate`. Therefore, you need to add the following to the `ViewController` class:

```
class ViewController: UIViewController, CLLocationManagerDelegate {
```

The `CLLocationManagerDelegate` protocol contains a number of methods that the conforming class can implement, including the following:

➤ `optional func locationManager(_ manager: CLLocationManager!, didUpdateLocations locations: [AnyObject]!)`—Fired when new location data is available

➤ `optional func locationManager(_ manager: CLLocationManager!, didFailWithError error: NSError!)`—Fired when the location manager is unable to retrieve the location value

In this case, if you want to display the obtained location, the `ViewController` class should implement the first method, as shown here:

```
import CoreLocation

class ViewController: UIViewController, CLLocationManagerDelegate {

    var lm: CLLocationManager!

    required init(coder aDecoder: NSCoder)
    {
        super.init(coder: aDecoder)
    }

    override func viewDidLoad() {
        super.viewDidLoad()

        lm = CLLocationManager()
        lm.delegate = self
```

```
        lm.desiredAccuracy = 0
        lm.distanceFilter = 0

        if (UIDevice.currentDevice().systemVersion as
            NSString).floatValue>=8.0 {

            //---request for foreground location use---
            lm.requestWhenInUseAuthorization()
        }

        lm.startUpdatingLocation()
    }

    func locationManager(manager: CLLocationManager!,
        didUpdateLocations locations: [AnyObject]!) {

            var newLocation = locations.last as CLLocation
            println("\(newLocation.coordinate.latitude)")
            println("\(newLocation.coordinate.longitude)")
            println("\(newLocation.horizontalAccuracy)")
    }
```

In the preceding example, the `locationManager()` method will be called whenever the Location Manager is able to obtain new locations.

> **NOTE** *The complete source code for this example is available for download at* www.wrox.com/go/beginningswift.

SUMMARY

In this chapter, you learned about protocols and delegates and the important role they play in your iOS and Mac OS X app development. In particular, you learned how to define a protocol so that a class conforming to it can implement all the necessary methods.

1. Consider the following protocol:

```
protocol SampleProtocol {
    init(someProperty1:String)
    var someProperty1:String {get set}
    var someProperty2:Int {get set}
    func doSomething()
}
```

   Create a class named `SomeClass` that conforms to `SampleProtocol`.

2. Consider the following protocol:

```
@objc protocol SampleDelegate {
    func event1()
    optional func event2()
}
```

   Modify the `SomeClass` created in question #1 to create a delegate of type `SampleDelegate`. In addition, when the `doSomething()` method is called, it should trigger the `event1()` and `event2()` methods.

3. Create a class called `EventHandler` that conforms to the `SampleDelegate` protocol.

4. Create an instance of `SomeClass` and handle the methods fired by it.

▶ **WHAT YOU LEARNED IN THIS CHAPTER**

TOPIC	KEY CONCEPTS
Protocol	A protocol is a blueprint of methods and properties. It describes what a class should have but does not provide any implementation.
Conforming to a protocol	A class that conforms to a protocol needs to provide the implementation as dictated by the protocol.
Optional methods in a protocol	Use the `@objc` tag to indicate to the compiler that your class is interoperating with Objective-C.
Conforming to multiple protocols	A class can conform to multiple protocols.
Compulsory initializer	Use the `required` keyword to ensure that all subclasses of a class also provide an implementation for the initializer.
Delegate	A delegate is an instance of a type (such as a class) that can handle the methods of a class or a structure. Think of a delegate as an event handler.

12

Generics

WHAT YOU WILL LEARN IN THIS CHAPTER:

➤ The motivation behind generics

➤ How to implement generic functions

➤ How to implement generic functions using multiple parameters

➤ How to specify type constraints in generics

➤ How to define generic classes

➤ How to define generic structures

➤ How to define generic extensions

➤ How to use generics in protocols

➤ Specifying requirements for generics in associated types

Most modern programming languages support a language feature known as generics, and Swift is no exception. Generics enable you to write highly reusable functions that can work with a variety of data types. With generics, you specify a placeholder for the data type that your generic code (functions, classes, structures, protocols, etc.) is working with. The actual data type to use is specified only at a later stage when the generic code is being used. In this chapter, you will learn about Swift's support for generics.

UNDERSTANDING GENERICS

Generics are one of the most important features of Swift. Generics are so important that most of the types and classes in Swift are created using them. The best way to understand generics is to look at an example.

Consider the following function:

```
func swapNums(inout item1:Int, inout item2:Int) {
    let temp = item1
    item1 = item2
    item2 = temp
}
```

The `swapNums()` function declares two `inout` parameters and exchanges their values. The following code snippet shows how to use the `swapNums()` function to swap the values of two `Int` variables:

```
var num1 = 5
var num2 = 6

println("\(num1), \(num2)")  //---5,6---
swapNums(&num1, &num2)
println("\(num1), \(num2)")  //---6,5---
```

Note that the `swapNums()` function only allows you to swap two integer values. If you want the function to swap two string variables, you need to create another function, as shown here:

```
func swapStrings(inout item1:String, inout item2:String) {
    let temp = item1
    item1 = item2
    item2 = temp
}
```

Both functions have the same implementation; only the type of variables you are dealing with is different. The same is true if you want to swap two `Double` values:

```
func swapDoubles(inout item1:Double, inout item2:Double) {
    let temp = item1
    item1 = item2
    item2 = temp
}
```

As you can see, creating separate functions for different data types creates a lot of duplication of code (and effort).

Using Generic Functions

Using generics, you could rewrite the `swapNums()`, `swapStrings()`, and `swapDoubles()` functions using a single generic function:

```
func swapItems<T>(inout item1:T, inout item2:T) {
    let temp = item1
```

```
        item1 = item2
        item2 = temp
    }
```

The generic version of the function looks almost the same as the other three functions, except that instead of specifying the type of arguments the function is expecting, you use `T` as the placeholder:

```
func swapItems<T>(inout item1:T, inout item2:T) {
```

In this example, `T` is just the placeholder for the actual data type; you are not limited to using `T` as the placeholder. Another common placeholder name is `ItemType`. If you use `ItemType` as the placeholder, then the function declaration would look like this:

```
func swapItems<ItemType>(inout item1:ItemType, inout item2:ItemType) {
```

You can now call the `swapItems()` function just as you would when you call the `swapNums()` function:

```
var num1 = 5
var num2 = 6
swapItems(&num1, &num2)
println("\(num1), \(num2)")    //---6, 5---
```

The compiler will infer from the type of `num1` when you call the `swapItems()` function, and in this case, `T` would be of type `Int`. Likewise, if you call the `swapItems()` function using arguments of type `String`, `T` would now be `String`:

```
var str1 = "blueberry"
var str2 = "apple"
println("\(str1), \(str2)")  //---blueberry, apple---
swapItems(&str1, &str2)
println("\(str1), \(str2)")  //---apple, blueberry---
```

The same behavior applies to `Double` types:

```
var price1 = 23.5
var price2 = 16.8
println("\(price1), \(price2)") //---23.5, 16.8---
swapItems(&price1, &price2)
println("\(price1), \(price2)") //---16.8, 23.5---
```

Multiple Type Parameters

The previous section showed the generic function with only one specific data type. In reality, you often have functions that accept arguments of multiple data types. For example, if you are writing a function that deals with `Dictionary` types, you have to deal with key-value pairs, as shown in the following function:

```
func addToDictionary(key:Int, value:String) {
    ...
}
```

In the preceding function stub, you have two parameters: one of type `Int` and one of type `String`. The generic version of this function would look like this:

```
func addToDictionary<KeyType, ValueType>(key:KeyType, value:ValueType){
    ...
}
```

Here, the `KeyType` and `ValueType` are placeholders for the actual data type that you will use.

Specifying Type Constraint

In the previous section, you saw that the `swapItems()` function could work with any data type, but sometimes it is necessary to enforce the types with which your generic function is able to work. Consider the following example:

```
func sortItems<T>(inout items:[T]) {
    for var j=0; j<items.count-1; j++ {
        var swapped = false
        for var i=0; i<items.count-1-j; i++ {
            if items[i]>items[i+1] {
                swapItems(&items[i], &items[i+1])
                swapped = true
            }
        }
        if !swapped {
            break
        }
    }
}
```

The preceding generic function implements the bubble sort algorithm for sorting an array of items. However, this code snippet will not compile. That's because you have a statement that performs comparison:

```
if items[i]>items[i+1] {
```

Because at compile time the compiler does not know the actual data type of the array that you would pass into the function, it generates an error, as some data types do not allow you to perform comparisons. Imagine passing in an array containing `Bool` values (`true` and `false`)—there is no way you can perform comparisons with Boolean values.

To fix this, you need to specify the constraint for the type that your function can accept:

```
func sortItems<T: Comparable>(inout items:[T]) {
    for var j=0; j<items.count-1; j++ {
        var swapped = false
        for var i=0; i<items.count-1; i++ {
            if items[i]>items[i+1] {
                swapItems(&items[i], &items[i+1])
                swapped = true
            }
    }
```

```
        if !swapped {
            break
        }
    }
}
```

In the preceding modifications, the highlighted statement reads *"any type T that conforms to the Comparable protocol."* In this case, it means that the function can only accept values of types that implement the `Comparable` protocol, which allows their values to be compared using the *less than operator* (>), *greater than operator* (<), and so on.

Besides the `Comparable` protocol, you can also specify the following protocols:

➤ `Equatable`—Makes it possible to determine whether two values are considered to be equal

➤ `Printable`—Enables you to customize the textual representation of any type ready for printing

Besides specifying the protocol that a type needs to implement, you can also specify a class type. For example, the following `doSomething()` function specifies that `T` must be an instance of the `MyCustomClass` class:

```
func doSomething<T:MyCustomClass>(obj:T) {
    ...
}
```

GENERIC TYPES

Generics are not limited to functions; you can also have generic types. Generic types can be any of the following:

➤ Classes

➤ Structures

➤ Protocols

Generic Classes

Consider the following example:

```
class MyIntStack {
    var elements = [Int]()
    func push(item:Int) {
        elements.append(item)
    }

    func pop() -> Int! {
        if elements.count>0 {
            return elements.removeLast()
        } else {
```

```
                    return nil
                }
            }
        }
```

The preceding code snippet is a classic implementation of a stack data structure in Swift. A stack data structure enables you to *push* (insert) and *pop* (remove) items in the Last-In-First-Out (LIFO) fashion. In the preceding implementation, MyIntStack is dealing only with the Int type. Observe that the pop() method returns a value of type Int! (implicit optional). This ensures that in the event that the stack is empty, a pop operation will simply return a nil value.

You can make use of MyIntStack as follows:

```
var myIntStack = MyIntStack()
myIntStack.push(5)
myIntStack.push(6)
myIntStack.push(7)
println(myIntStack.pop())   //---7---
println(myIntStack.pop())   //---6---
println(myIntStack.pop())   //---5---
println(myIntStack.pop())   //---nil---
```

You could rewrite the class as a generic class:

```
class MyStack<T> {
    var elements = [T]()
    func push(item:T) {
        elements.append(item)
    }

    func pop() -> T! {
        if elements.count>0 {
            return elements.removeLast()
        } else {
            return nil
        }
    }
}
```

To use the MyStack class for Int values, simply specify the data type enclosed with angle brackets (<>) during instantiation of the class:

```
var myIntStack = MyStack<Int>()
```

You can now use the class as usual:

```
myIntStack.push(5)
myIntStack.push(6)
myIntStack.push(7)
println(myIntStack.pop())       //---7---
println(myIntStack.pop())       //---6---
println(myIntStack.pop())       //---5---
println(myIntStack.pop())       //---nil---
```

You can also use the `MyStack` class with the `String` type:

```
var myStringStack = MyStack<String>()
myStringStack.push("Programming")
myStringStack.push("Swift")
println(myStringStack.pop())   //---Swift---
println(myStringStack.pop())   //---Programming---
println(myStringStack.pop())   //---nil---
```

Generic Structures

In the previous section you saw the use of generics in classes. Generics also apply to structures. Consider the following implementation of a *queue* using a structure:

```
struct MyIntQueue {
    var elements = [Int]()
    var startIndex = 0

    mutating func queue(item: Int) {
        elements.append(item)
    }

    mutating func dequeue() -> Int! {
        if elements.isEmpty {
            return nil
        } else {
            return elements.removeAtIndex(0)
        }
    }
}
```

A queue is a data structure that allows you to *queue* (insert) and *dequeue* (retrieve) items. In the preceding implementation, `MyIntQueue` deals only with the `Int` type. You can use it as follows:

```
var myIntQueue = MyIntQueue()
myIntQueue.queue(7)
myIntQueue.queue(8)
println(myIntQueue.dequeue())   //---7---
println(myIntQueue.dequeue())   //---8---
println(myIntQueue.dequeue())   //---nil---
```

Rewriting the current implementation to use generics yields the following structure:

```
struct MyGenericQueue<T> {
    var elements = [T]()
    var startIndex = 0

    mutating func queue(item: T) {
        elements.append(item)
    }

    mutating func dequeue() -> T! {
        if elements.isEmpty {
```

```
            return nil
        } else {
            return elements.removeAtIndex(0)
        }
    }
}
```

You can now use the `MyGenericQueue` structure for any specified data type:

```
var myGenericQueue = MyGenericQueue<String>()
myGenericQueue.queue("Hello")
myGenericQueue.queue("Swift")
println(myGenericQueue.dequeue())   //---Hello---
println(myGenericQueue.dequeue())   //---Swift---
println(myGenericQueue.dequeue())   //---nil---
```

Generic Type Extension

Recall that earlier we had a generic stack class:

```
class MyStack<T> {
    var elements = [T]()
    func push(item:T) {
        elements.append(item)
    }

    func pop() -> T! {
        if elements.count>0 {
            return elements.removeLast()
        } else {
            return nil
        }
    }
}
```

When you extend a generic type, the parameter list in the original type definition is available in the extension. In the preceding class, T is the placeholder name for the parameter type—you can write an extension for the `MyStack` class and it would also be available in the extension:

```
extension MyStack {
    func peek(position:Int) -> T! {
        if position<0 || position>elements.count-1 {
            return nil
        } else {
            return elements[position]
        }
    }
}
```

The preceding extension adds the `peek()` method to the `MyStack` class, enabling users to examine elements of the stack by specifying their position, without removing them.

The following code snippet shows how to use the new `peek()` extension method that you have just added:

```
var myStack = MyStack<String>()

myStack.push("The")
myStack.push("Quick")
myStack.push("Brown")
myStack.push("Fox")

println(myStack.peek(0)) //---The---
println(myStack.peek(1)) //---Quick---
println(myStack.peek(2)) //---Brown---

println(myStack.pop())    //---Fox---
println(myStack.pop())    //---Brown---
println(myStack.pop())    //---Quick---
println(myStack.pop())    //---The---
```

Using Generics in Protocols

Generics can also be applied to protocols.

> **NOTE** Protocols are discussed in detail in Chapter 11.

Consider the following `MyStackProtocol` protocol:

```
protocol MyStackProtocol {
    typealias T
    func push(item:T)
    func pop() -> T!
    func peek(position:Int) -> T!
}
```

In this example, the `MyStackProtocol` protocol specifies that any class that wants to implement a stack data structure needs to implement three methods:

➤ `push()`—Accepts an argument of type `T`

➤ `pop()`—Returns an item of type `T`

➤ `peek()`—Accepts an integer argument and returns an item of type `T`

The protocol does not dictate how elements in the stack are to be stored—one implementation can use an array, while another can use a double-linked list, for example. Because the protocol does not dictate the data type that the stack needs to deal with, it declares an *associated type* using the `typealias` keyword:

```
typealias T
```

The T is the placeholder for the actual data type that would be used by the implementer of this protocol.

When implementing the protocol, you need to implement the required methods declared in the protocol in your implementing class. The following code snippet shows one example:

```
class MyOwnStack: MyStackProtocol {

    typealias T = String

    var elements = [String]()

    func push(item:String) {
        elements.append(item)
    }

    func pop() -> String! {
        if elements.count>0 {
            return elements.removeLast()
        } else {
            return nil
        }
    }

    func peek(position:Int) -> String! {
        if position<0 || position>elements.count-1 {
            return nil
        } else {
            return elements[position]
        }
    }
}
```

Here, the MyOwnStack class conforms to the MyStackProtocol protocol. Because you are now implementing a stack to manipulate String types, you assign T to String, as shown here:

```
    typealias T = String
```

In fact, there is no need to explicitly declare the preceding statement; the type of T can be inferred from the implementation:

```
    func push(item:String) {      //---type of item is String---
        elements.append(item)
    }
```

The MyOwnStack class can now be rewritten like this:

```
class MyOwnStack: MyStackProtocol {

    var elements = [String]()

    func push(item:String) {
```

```
        elements.append(item)
    }

    func pop() -> String! {
        if elements.count>0 {
            return elements.removeLast()
        } else {
            return nil
        }
    }

    func peek(position:Int) -> String! {
        if position<0 || position>elements.count-1 {
            return nil
        } else {
            return elements[position]
        }
    }
}
```

You can use the `MyOwnStack` class as follows:

```
var myOwnStack = MyOwnStack()
myOwnStack.push("Swift")
myOwnStack.push("Hello")
println(myOwnStack.pop())    //---Hello---
println(myOwnStack.pop())    //---Swift ---
```

However, because we are talking about generics in this chapter, the `MyOwnStack` class should ideally be a generic class as well. Here is the generic implementation of the `MyOwnStackProtocol` protocol:

```
class MyOwnGenericStack<T>: MyStackProtocol {
    var elements = [T]()

    func push(item:T) {
        elements.append(item)
    }

    func pop() -> T! {
        if elements.count>0 {
            return elements.removeLast()
        } else {
            return nil
        }
    }

    func peek(position:Int) -> T! {
        if position<0 || position>elements.count-1 {
            return nil
        } else {
            return elements[position]
        }
    }
}
```

You can now use the `MyOwnGenericStack` class as follows:

```
var myOwnGenericStack = MyOwnGenericStack<String>()
myOwnGenericStack.push("Swift")
myOwnGenericStack.push("Hello")
println(myOwnGenericStack.pop())    //---Hello---
println(myOwnGenericStack.pop())    //---Swift---
```

Specifying Requirements for Associated Types

Suppose you have a function that compares two stacks to determine whether they are equal (i.e., have the same elements and count). Your function might look like this:

```
func compareMyStacks
    <ItemType1:MyStackProtocol, ItemType2:MyStackProtocol>
    (stack1: ItemType1, stack2:ItemType2) -> Bool {

    ...
    return true
}
```

In the `compareMyStacks()` function, you specified it as a generic function that takes two stacks as arguments, first of `ItemType1` and second of `ItemType2`. These two types must conform to the `MyStackProtocol` protocol. A use of the `compareMyStacks()` function might look like this:

```
var myOwnGenericStack1 = MyOwnGenericStack<String>()
var myOwnGenericStack2 = MyOwnGenericStack<String>()
var same =
    compareMyStacks(myOwnGenericStack1, stack2:myOwnGenericStack2)
```

In this case, because both stacks (`myOwnGenericStack1` and `myOwnGenericStack2`) use the `String` type, the comparison can be performed. However, what if you want to compare stacks of different types? In this case it is not possible to perform the comparison, and you need to enforce this restriction based on the type acceptable to the `compareMyStacks()` function. You can do so by specifying a `where` condition:

```
func compareMyStacks
    <ItemType1:MyStackProtocol, ItemType2:MyStackProtocol
    where ItemType1.T == ItemType2.T>
    (stack1: ItemType1, stack2:ItemType2) -> Bool {

    ...
    return true
}
```

In the preceding statement, the `where` condition dictates that the type used by the two arguments (which conforms to the `MyStackProtocol` protocol) must be the same. If you now try to compare two stacks of different types, the compiler will generate an error:

```
var myOwnGenericStack2 = MyOwnGenericStack<String>()
var myOwnGenericStack3 = MyOwnGenericStack<Double>()

//---error---
compareMyStacks(myOwnGenericStack2, stack2: myOwnGenericStack3)
```

In the preceding code snippet, `myOwnGenericStack2` uses the `String` type and `myOwnGenericStack3` uses the `Double` type. Hence, passing them as arguments to the `compareMyStacks()` function violates the `where` clause.

In addition to ensuring that the type for the two arguments is the same, you may also need to enforce the constraint that the arguments are of a specific type, such as those that conform to the `Comparable` protocol:

```
func compareMyStacks<
    ItemType1:MyStackProtocol, ItemType2:MyStackProtocol
    where ItemType1.T == ItemType2.T, ItemType1.T:Comparable>
    (stack1: ItemType1, stack2:ItemType2) -> Bool {
    ...
    return true
}
```

Once you have specified this constraint, you will not be able to compare stacks that use the `Bool` type (the `Bool` type does not conform to the `Comparable` protocol):

```
var myOwnGenericStack4 = MyOwnGenericStack<Bool>()
var myOwnGenericStack5 = MyOwnGenericStack<Bool>()

//---error---
compareMyStacks(myOwnGenericStack4, stack2: myOwnGenericStack5)
```

> **NOTE** *The actual implementation of the* `compareMyStacks()` *function is left as an exercise for the reader.*

SUMMARY

In this chapter, you learned about a very important topic in Swift—generics. Generics enable your code to be highly flexible and reusable. You saw how generics can be applied to classes, structures, and extensions, as well as protocols. In addition, type constraints can be applied to generics.

EXERCISES

1. Given the following protocol, add a function to it to return the count of elements within the stack:

```
protocol MyStackProtocol {
    typealias T
    func push(item:T)
    func pop() -> T!
    func peek(position:Int) -> T!
}
```

2. Given the following class that conforms to the `MyStackProtocol`, implement the function that you have added to the protocol in question #1:

```
class MyOwnGenericStack<T>: MyStackProtocol {
    var elements = [T]()

    func push(item:T) {
        elements.append(item)
    }

    func pop() -> T! {
        if elements.count>0 {
            return elements.removeLast()
        } else {
            return nil
        }
    }

    func peek(position:Int) -> T! {
        if position<0 || position>elements.count-1 {
            return nil
        } else {
            return elements[position]
        }
    }
}
```

3. Implement a function that compares two instances of the `MyOwnGenericStack` class as shown in question #2, and return `true` if both stacks are the same and `false` if they are not the same.

▶ **WHAT YOU LEARNED IN THIS CHAPTER**

TOPIC	KEY CONCEPTS
Generics	Generics is a way of coding in which functions are written in terms of placeholder types that are later replaced with specific types provided as parameters.
Advantage of generics	Generics facilitate code reuse.
Protocols for specifying type constraints	Some protocols include `Comparable`, `Equatable`, and `Printable`.
Generic types	Generics are also applicable to classes, structures, and protocols.
Generic type extension	You can extend a generic type.
Specifying requirements for associated types	Allows you to specify the relationships between two generic types.

APPENDIX

Exercise Answers

CHAPTER 1

Exercise 1

```
let months = 12
let daysInWeek = 7
let weeks = 52
```

Exercise 2

```
var gender = "Female"
var weight = 102.5      // in pounds
var height = 1.72       // in meters
var DOB = "09/25/1970"  // mm/dd/yyyy
```

Exercise 3

```
println("Gender: \(gender)")
println("Weight: \(weight) pounds")
println("Height: \(height) meters")
println("DOB: \(DOB)")
```

Exercise 4

```
var weight = 102.5      // in pounds
var str = "Your weight is \(weight) pounds"
```

CHAPTER 2

Exercise 1

The problem with the code is that weightInPounds is inferred to be of type Int, which will cause the error when using it to multiply other Double values.

The first way to fix this is to ensure that you assign a floating-point value to weightInPounds so that the compiler can infer it to be of type Double:

```
var weightInPounds = 154.0
var heightInInches = 66.9
var BMI = (weightInPounds / pow(heightInInches,2)) * 703.06957964
println(BMI)
```

The second approach is to explicitly declare weightInPounds as a Double:

```
var weightInPounds:Double = 154
var heightInInches = 66.9
var BMI = (weightInPounds / pow(heightInInches,2)) * 703.06957964
println(BMI)
```

The third approach is to explicitly perform a cast on weightInPounds and heightInInches when performing the calculations:

```
var weightInPounds = 154
var heightInInches = 66.9
var BMI = (Double(weightInPounds) / pow(Double(heightInInches),2)) * 703.06957964
println(BMI)
```

Exercise 2

The output for the following statements is as follows. (The statements in bold are the values implicitly assigned by the compiler.)

```
enum cartoonCharacters: Int {
    case FelixTheCat = 1
    case AngelicaPickles    // = 2
    case ThePowerpuffGirls  // = 3
    case SpiderMan = 9
    case GeorgeOfTheJungle  // = 10
    case Superman           // = 11
    case Batman             // = 12
}

var d = cartoonCharacters.GeorgeOfTheJungle
println(d.rawValue)    //---prints out 10---

d = cartoonCharacters.AngelicaPickles
println(d.rawValue)    //---prints out 2---
```

Exercise 3

The output for the following statements is as follows. (The statements in bold are the values implicitly assigned by the compiler.)

```
enum cartoonCharacters: Int {
    case FelixTheCat        // = 0
    case AngelicaPickles    // = 1
    case ThePowerpuffGirls  // = 2
    case SpiderMan = 9
    case GeorgeOfTheJungle  // = 10
    case Superman           // = 11
    case Batman             // = 12
}

var d = cartoonCharacters.GeorgeOfTheJungle
println(d.rawValue)    //---prints out 10---

d = cartoonCharacters.AngelicaPickles
println(d.rawValue)    //---prints out 1---
```

Exercise 4

You should ensure that isMember is not nil before using it. Then unwrap it using the ! character:

```
var isMember:Bool?
if isMember != nil {
    if isMember! {
        println("User is a member")
    } else {
        println("User is a not member")
    }
}
```

CHAPTER 3

Exercise 1

You can use the find () function together with the distance () function to obtain the position of the "q" character:

```
var str1 = "The quick brown fox jumps over the lazy dog"
let char:Character = "q"
if let charIndex = find(str1, char) {
    let charPosition = distance(str1.startIndex, charIndex)
    println(charPosition)   //---4---
}
```

Exercise 2

You can cast the strings as `NSString` first and then use the `doubleValue` property to extract their double values:

```
var amount = "1200"
var rate = "1.27"
var result = (amount as NSString).doubleValue *
             (rate as NSString).doubleValue
```

Exercise 3

You can use the string interpolation method to include `Double` values in your output:

```
var lat = 40.765819
var lng = -73.975866
println("Lat/Lng is (\(lat), \(lng))")
```

CHAPTER 4

Exercise 1

```
var num = 5
var sum = ++num + num++

println(num)    //---7---
println(sum)    //---12---
```

Exercise 2

```
var nums = [3,4,2,1,5,7,9,8]
var sumOfOdds = 0
for i in 0 ..< nums.count {
    if nums[i] % 2 == 1 {
        sumOfOdds += nums[i]
    }
}
println(sumOfOdds)
```

Exercise 3

```
var userInput = "5"
var num = userInput.toInt()
var value = num ?? 0
```

CHAPTER 5

Exercise 1

```
func countNumbers(string: String) -> (odd:Int, even:Int, threes:Int) {
    var odd = 0, even = 0, threes = 0
    for char in string {
        let digit = String(char).toInt()
        if (digit != nil) {
            (digit!) % 2 == 0 ? even++ : odd++
            (digit!) % 3 == 0 ? threes++ : 0
        }
    }
    return (odd, even, threes)
}

    var result = countNumbers("123456789")
    println("Odd: \(result.odd)")        //---5---
    println("Even: \(result.even)")      //---4---
    println("Threes: \(result.threes)")  //---3---
```

Exercise 2

```
func doSomething(arg1:String, #withSomething:String) {

}
```

Exercise 3

```
func sum(nums: Int...) -> Int {
    var sum = 0
    for num in nums {
        sum += num
    }
    return sum
}
```

Exercise 4

```
func cat(joiner:String = " ", nums: Int...) -> String {
    var str = ""
    for (index, num) in enumerate(nums) {
        str = str + String(num)
        if index != nums.count - 1 {
            str += joiner
        }
    }
    return str
}
```

CHAPTER 6

Exercise 1

```
var nums = [1,2,3,4,5,6,7,8,9]
for num in nums {
    if num % 2 == 0 {
        println(num)
    }
}
```

Exercise 2

```
var userInfo = Dictionary<String, String>()
userInfo["username"] = "weimenglee"
userInfo["password"] = "secret"
userInfo["dob"] = "31/01/1960"
```

Exercise 3

```
for product in products {
    println(product.0)
    println("========")
    var models = product.1
    for model in models {
        println(model)
    }
    println()
}
```

CHAPTER 7

Exercise 1

```
func Fibonacci(num:Int) -> Int {
    if num <= 1 {
        return 1
    }
    return Fibonacci(num - 1) + Fibonacci(num - 2)
}

//---prints out the first 13 Fibonacci numbers---
for i in 0...12 {
    println(Fibonacci(i))
}
```

Exercise 2

```
func GCD(var a: Int, var b: Int) -> Int
{
    var remainder = 0
    while( b != 0 ) {
        remainder = a % b
        a = b
        b = remainder
    }
    return a
}

println(GCD(12,b:8))   //---4---
```

Exercise 3

```
func isPrime(num: Int) -> Bool {
    var prime = true
    var factor = pow(Double(num), 0.5)
    for var i = 2; i <= Int(factor); i++ {
        if (num % i) == 0 {
            prime = false
        }
    }
    return prime
}

for i in 2...1000 {
    if isPrime(i) {
        println("\(i) is prime")
    }
}
```

CHAPTER 8

Exercise 1

```
struct DOB {
    var year: Int
    var month: Int
    var day: Int
}
```

Exercise 2

```
struct Student {
    var ID: String
    var name: String
    var dob: DOB
}
```

Exercise 3

```
struct Student {
    var ID: String
    var name: String
    var dob: DOB
    var age: Int {
        get {
            let date = NSDate()
            let calendar = NSCalendar.currentCalendar()
            let components = calendar.components(
                NSCalendarUnit.YearCalendarUnit |
                NSCalendarUnit.MonthCalendarUnit, fromDate: date)
            return components.year - self.dob.year
        }
    }
}
```

Exercise 4

```
var student1 = Student(
    ID: "12345",
    name: "Chloe Lee",
    dob: DOB(
        year: 2010,
        month: 1,
        day: 31))
```

Exercise 5

```
println(student1.age)
```

CHAPTER 9

Exercise 1

```
enum Color: String {
    case Red = "Red"
    case Blue = "Blue"
    case White = "white"
}

class Vehicle {
    var model: String
    var doors: Int
    var color: Color
    var wheels: Int

    init() {
```

```
        model = ""
        doors = 0
        color = Color.White
        wheels = 0
    }
}
```

Exercise 2

```
class MotorVehicle: Vehicle {
    var licensePlate: String

    override init() {
        licensePlate = "NOT ASSIGNED"
        super.init()
    }
}
```

Exercise 3

```
class Bicycle: Vehicle {
    override init() {
        super.init()
        wheels = 2
        doors = 0
    }
}
```

Exercise 4

```
class Car: MotorVehicle {
    override init() {
        super.init()
        doors = 2
    }

    init(model:String, doors:Int, color:Color, wheels: Int) {
        super.init()
        self.model = model
        self.doors = doors
        self.color = color
        self.wheels = wheels
    }

    convenience init(licensePlate:String) {
        self.init(model:"", doors:2, color:Color.White, wheels:2)
        self.licensePlate = licensePlate
    }
}
```

CHAPTER 10

Exercise 1

```
let numNames = [
    0: "Zero",
    1: "One",
    2: "Two",
    3: "Three",
    4: "Four",
    5: "Five",
    6: "Six",
    7: "Seven",
    8: "Eight",
    9: "Nine"
]
var numbers = [5,6,3,2,4,8,1,0]
var numbersNames = numbers.map(
    {
        (num: Int) -> String in
            return numNames[num]!
    }
)
println(numbersNames)
```

Exercise 2

```
var oddNumbers = numbers.filter(
    {
        (num: Int) -> Bool in
            num % 2 == 1
    }
)
println(oddNumbers)//---[5, 3, 1]---
```

Exercise 3

```
var biggestNumber = numbers.reduce(
    numbers[0],
    {
        (maxNum: Int, num: Int) -> Int in
        return max(maxNum, num)
    }
)
println(biggestNumber)  //---8---
```

Exercise 4

```
var sum = numbers.reduce(
    0,
    {
        (sum: Int, num: Int) -> Int in
```

```
                        return sum + num
                }
        )
        var average = Double(sum) / Double(numbers.count)
        println(average)
```

CHAPTER 11

Exercise 1

```
class SomeClass:SampleProtocol {
    var someProperty1:String
    var someProperty2:Int

    required init(someProperty1:String) {
        self.someProperty1 = someProperty1
        self.someProperty2 = 0
    }

    func doSomething() {
    }
}
```

Exercise 2

```
class SomeClass:SampleProtocol {
    var someProperty1:String
    var someProperty2:Int

    var delegate:SampleDelegate?

    required init(someProperty1:String) {
        self.someProperty1 = someProperty1
        self.someProperty2 = 0
    }

    func doSomething() {
        delegate?.event1()
        delegate?.event2?()
        //---you need the ? after event2() as it is optional---
    }
}
```

Exercise 3

```
class EventHandler:SampleDelegate {
    func event1() {
        println("event1 handled")
    }
    func event2() {
```

```
                    println("event2 handled")
            }
    }

```

Exercise 4

```
class EventHandler:SampleDelegate {
    func event1() {
            println("event1 handled")
    }
    func event2() {
            println("event2 handled")
    }
}

var eventHandler = EventHandler()
var sc = SomeClass(someProperty1:"something")
sc.delegate = eventHandler
sc.doSomething()
```

CHAPTER 12

Exercise 1

```
protocol MyStackProtocol {
    typealias T
    func push(item:T)
    func pop() -> T!
    func peek(position:Int) -> T!
    func count() -> Int
}
```

Exercise 2

```
class MyOwnGenericStack<T>: MyStackProtocol {
    var elements = [T]()

    func push(item:T) {
        elements.append(item)
    }

    func pop() -> T! {
        if elements.count>0 {
            return elements.removeLast()
        } else {
            return nil
        }
    }

    func peek(position:Int) -> T! {
```

```
            if position<0 || position>elements.count-1 {
                return nil
            } else {
                return elements[position]
            }
        }

    func count() -> Int {
        return elements.count
    }
}
```

Exercise 3

```
func compareMyStacks
    <ItemType1:MyStackProtocol, ItemType2:MyStackProtocol where
        ItemType1.T == ItemType2.T, ItemType1.T:Comparable>
    (stack1: ItemType1, stack2:ItemType2) -> Bool {

    //---if both stacks are empty---
    if stack1.count() == 0 && stack2.count() == 0 {
        return true
    }

    //---if the size of both stacks are not the same---
    if stack1.count() != stack2.count() {
        return false
    }

    //---compare each element in the stack---
    for i in 0 ..< stack1.count() {
        if stack1.peek(i)! != stack2.peek(i)! {
            return false
        }
    }
    return true
}
```

INDEX